SKILLS ARE CHEAP PASSION IS PRICELESS

Turn Your Passion Into

Unstoppable Profit Making Machine

RHONDA SWAN

https://unstoppablemomma.com

For FREE Book Bonuses and Video Training

Go to https://unstoppablemomma.com/bonus

DISCLAIMER

Skills Are Cheap, Passion Is Priceless

Copyright © 2016, Rhonda Swan

All Rights Reserved

First published 2016

All rights reserved. Without limiting the rights under copyright reserved above, no part of this publication may be reproduced, stored in or introduced into a database and retrieval system or transmitted in any form or any means (electronic, mechanical, photocopying, recording or otherwise) without the prior written permission of both the owner of copyright and the publishers.

The people, events and information contained within this Book is strictly for educational purposes. If you wish to apply ideas contained in this Book, you are taking full responsibility for your actions.

All rights reserved

First Edition

Published by Digital Publishing Australia

ISBN - 9781540468963

Table of Contents

Dedication & Acknowledgements

This book is dedicated to all the parents with a 'WHY' to raise their children and keep them out of day care. The dreamers, the visionaries and those crazy enough to go after their dreams and live a life of FREEDOM.

To the 'Unstoppable Tribe of Freedom-Preneurs" that we have met and worked with from around the world. Each of you have inspired us to continue after our dreams and stay true to our vision of Freedom.

There are several people I would like to thank who've played a key role in our journey of entrepreneurialism that have led to where we are today.

Jubril Agoro, friend, family, business partner, mentor and 'Uncle Bril' to Hanalei. Our journey over the last 10 years has been the wildest roller coaster ride of highs, lows and everything in between. From the 'El Cortez' to traveling around the world together, we have gone through it all and are excited for what has yet to come for you.

My parents, who still have no idea 'what I do', thank you for your support and true love throughout the years.

Dan Usher for putting his heart and soul into our promotional videos and films, you are cherished and appreciated.

Mentors from afar who have changed our thinking and the way we conduct business; Tim Ferriss, Cynthia Kersey, Wayne Dyer, Deepak Chopra and Lisa Sasevich to name a few.

Foreword

My entrepreneurial journey started for one reason ... and then turned into a search for accolades and awards, recognition and fame. Instead, I found frustration and disillusionment, not realizing this search was actually keeping me from the very thing I sought.

For years, I seethed with envy, watching other business owners and marketers succeed while I spun my wheels. As jealousy turned to resentment, I began to see the world through murky-colored glasses, finding fault with everything these people did.

And for a while, this feeling consumed me. However, eventually I had to come to grips with reality: being jaded was doing me absolutely no good.

I didn't become a better marketer.

I didn't become famous.

I didn't get a book published.

I didn't make any more money.

After years of feeling this way, I decided to make a change: Instead of letting external factors dictate my success, I would focus on what I could control: my attitude.

Tip #1: Focus on passion, not results.

At first, nothing changed. I was doing my work, the same as I ever was. But internally, I was changing. Instead of a paycheck or pat on the back, passion was now my most important metric.

If I showed up to my business - for love, not accolades - then I had done my job. At least for that day, I'd succeeded. And tomorrow was another day.

This released me up from the pressure to perform, gave me greater artistic freedom, and made my work a lot more fun.

If nobody but me showed up to read my blog posts, I would still write them.

If no one watched my video I would still shoot them.

If I never got a lead, I would still market my business.

If I never earned a dime, I would still build my business.

Tip #2: Do your best work when nobody's watching.

Wait a second. Isn't that ironic?

Aren't you trying to get us to watch this video, work with you or buy your book?

But there's a paradox in the pursuit of fame: those who try the hardest to earn others' attention rarely get it.

Conversely, those who scorn the limelight are often the ones dodging the paparazzi.

Of course, this isn't always the case. But with online marketing and other artistic crafts, I've found it to be undeniably accurate. Something interesting happens when you make passion your chief pursuit:

People start to notice.

The world is desperate for, even envious of, people living purposeful lives that are free from fear. We are all inspired by those brave enough to shirk the trappings of fame and do work that matters.

What happens every time you see a film or read a book about some hero who risks it all to complete a quest that matters? You're inspired. Captivated, even.

When I began building my business for passion, at first nobody seemed to care. But I kept at it, kept doing the best work I could no matter how many (or how few) paid attention. And slowly over time, people took notice.

Why? Because there is something attractive about passion.

Tip #3: The less you care about your audience's affections, the more your audience will be affected by your work.

Don't do it for the money!

I've talked to dozens of successful marketers, authors, and entrepreneurs about why they do what they do. And they've all told me essentially the same thing: It's not about the money.

Billionaire Donald Trump once said:

'Money was never a big motivation for me, except as a way to keep score.

The real excitement is playing the game.'

If you're setting out to master a craft, to play your own game, maybe you hope to someday become famous or rich. But if you were to dig a little deeper, you might find that such a goal isn't what you're really in search of.

Of course, there's nothing inherently wrong with money or the acquisition of it. Nor is there anything immoral about wanting a large audience or a best-selling book. It's just that those things aren't enough to fulfill you.

Because what happens on the days when nobody shows up to watch your work, or experience your art? Do you still continue?

Not if it's about the rewards.

Passion and creation is a process, not a product.

Our work is more than what we do or make. It's the entirety of effort that goes into each step of the process. In a sense, it's what we don't see.

So when you're sweating and bleeding and loving every minute of it, remember: this is the reward.

What, do you do, then, when you create something you're proud of and people don't appreciate it? Do you quit? Give up because your work isn't 'relevant'? Or do you push forward, remembering that history's greatest artists were often misunderstood by contemporaries?

The most memorable creations are rarely comprehended by the masses - at first.

This is what makes passion so attractive. It exceeds our expectations and sometimes offends our sensibilities.

Take heart, though. Someday, someone will get it. And they will be transformed. Until then, you must learn to love the work.

Tip #4: Respect the process, and results will come.

Isn't it ironic?

You know, the Greeks didn't write obituaries. They only asked one question after a man died: 'Did he have passion?'

When we set sail in search of our life's work, this is what we must seek: passion.

Not fame or rewards or riches, but a willingness to quietly do our work, trusting the sowing-and-reaping nature of life. Remembering that good things come in time if we do our jobs well.

So where does that leave us? Where, practically, can you go from here? Strive to do your work with gratitude and generosity.

Because this part is not you paying your dues or delaying gratification until payday. This is the best it gets.

The grind is the reward.

And if you aren't okay with that, then quit now. Because it's only once you've mastered this mindset that you'll have any shot at making it, at getting rich and famous.

What this meant for me was admitting that building online businesses and branding was my passion, something I couldn't not do. And truth be told, when I was doing it for the wrong reasons, I knew it. Constantly anxious and uneasy, I worked with apprehension. It felt unnatural.

Only when I surrendered to the work, did I find peace - and my audience. And maybe as you chase your passion, you'll make a similar discovery and allow passion to drive you over success.

Inside this book "Skills Are Cheap, Passion Is Priceless" I walk you through the process I took to find this self-discovery of living Unstoppable with passion and purpose. Enjoy!

Unstoppable Action Steps

If money was no object and you could do anything, what would you do?

____

____

____

What is your passion, what makes your heart sing?

____

____

____

Go to Facebook group and share – www.facebook.com/groups/1FreedomPreneur/

We have sooooo many FREE resources to help you with this at

https://unstoppablemomma.com/bonus for your FREE book resources to help you.

PART ONE:
OUR STORY

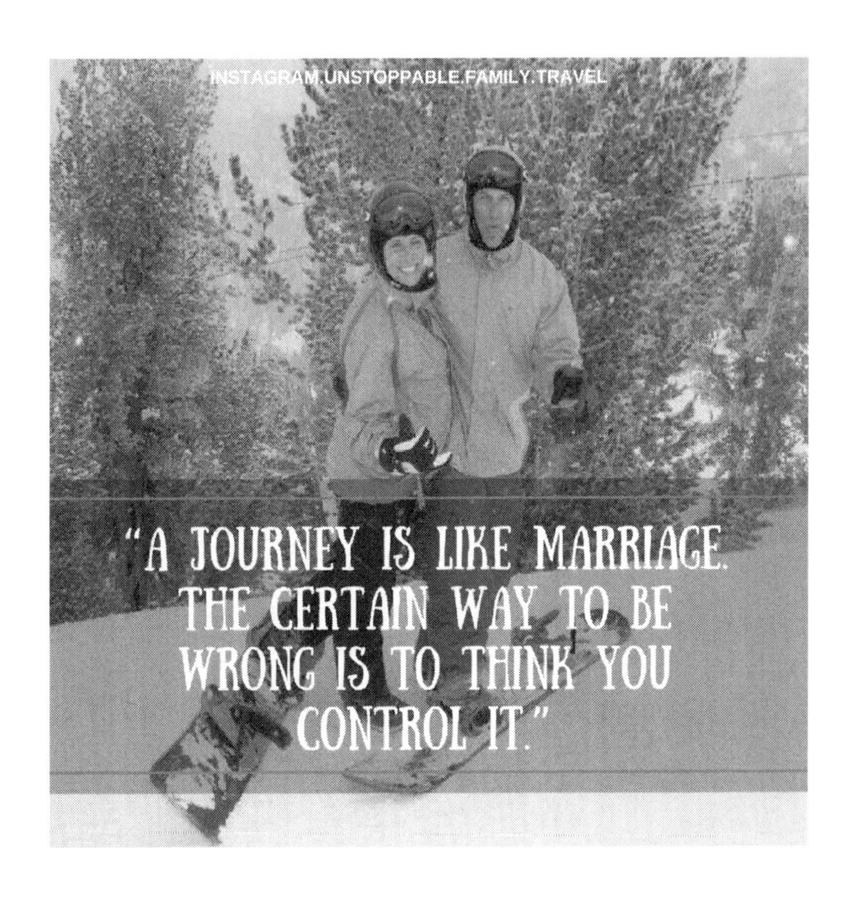
INSTAGRAM.UNSTOPPABLE.FAMILY.TRAVEL
"A JOURNEY IS LIKE MARRIAGE.
THE CERTAIN WAY TO BE
WRONG IS TO THINK YOU
CONTROL IT."

1

Early Years: Drugs, Alcohol & A Product Of The 70's

"What we think determines what happens to us,

so if we want to change our lives,

we need to stretch our minds."

~ Wayne Dyer

Who would have ever thought, a blue collar family girl from Michigan set out with a dream to climb the ladder of a large corporation would be celebrating her 8th year of traveling the world with her family. But it wasn't always like this ... allow me to give you some background of my life that has led me to this point of being UNSTOPPABLE. My name is Rhonda Swan, and ***I am Unstoppable***. Everything that has happened in my life has led me to this point and has made me unstoppable. Because of this realization, I thought it was about time that I share with you the story that has led me to this point.

I was born to an amazingly strong woman originally known as Barbara Samples. She was brought up in Michigan, Detroit, by her Mother and Father. My Grandfather who I have always called, Paw Paw, worked in the automotive industry, and my Granny raised eight children.

My Mom met my Father (and I will refer to him as my Father throughout because he was not a Dad to me in any sense of the word), John Saunders when they were both 19 years old. I was conceived, and they were married by the time they turned 20. You could say the beginning of their life together, and the start of my life as a whole was not very well planned or thought out.

I was born in '73, so I was raised in the 1970's generation and era. Or as I like to call it the 'Free Bird Era' because that is how I think of my Mom. My Mom was very young and naive when she met my Father who was somewhat more experienced and advanced. He had super high energy and was always running around after something and he loved to play baseball. He was even offered a professional position as a younger man, and life would have been very different if he had taken up the offer. But even then he was a 'fuck up' kind of guy, all talent and no focus. In all honesty, it had a lot to do with his upbringing; he didn't have a lot of structure, security or control in his family and that made him flighty and too nervous to settle down.

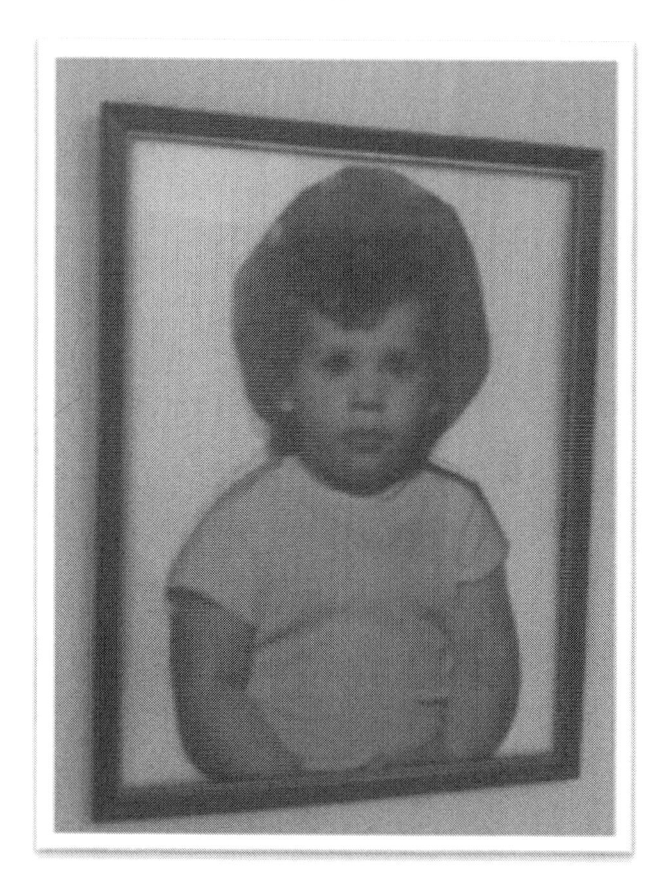

In the end, he turned to drugs, alcohol and partying to the cost of all else, even us. He brought my Mom along for the ride for a while, and she willingly followed because she was young and naive and had never experienced so much excitement before in her life.

Then I was born. There was my mom, only a young girl herself with a baby and a free flying crazy husband who was unpredictable at best and utterly reckless and dangerous in reality. The whole process, from conception and marriage to divorce, took only two years. Two years of constant chaos but only two years nonetheless.

I can still remember that my Paw Paw was always trying to chase my dad away with a gun. He was always trying to chase him away from the house, from his daughter and his Granddaughter with a gun! I can't blame my Paw Paw for these actions; he is a proud man, and my father had some ridiculous and unforgivable behavior. Like, he would take me grocery shopping and try to steal meat under the baby car seat, implicating me, even at that early age, into thievery. He got my Mom sent to jail several times, through his actions and cowardice. He would run off with his buddies and leave my Mom to deal with the trouble they had caused without a second thought to anyone else but his own happiness and freedom.

It didn't take my Mom long to realize that she couldn't be with him anymore if she wanted to have any future. She divorced my father in '75 and we went to live with my Grandparents. They were a very traditional Southern family. My Paw Paw was a Cherokee Indian, a huge, broad, imposing man and my Granny was a beautiful southern lady, very proper and hard working all her life. They were originally from Tennessee and embodied everything there was about Southern hospitality, raising a family and work ethic.

The whole time we lived with my Grandparents, it was a constant struggle with interruptions and explosions from my father. Throughout my entire life, in fact, knowing him has been like being on a roller coaster. Ups and downs together, never knowing if he would show up - alive or dead. He was heavily into drugs, so you never knew what news was coming next. My Paw Paw hated him with a vengeance.

I can vividly remember one incident when I had been with my father for the weekend, and he brought me back home to my grandparent's house. My Mom and Granny were sitting out the front of the house when we arrived home. I think I was about 4 or 5 at the time, and as we walked up to the front door my very proper southern Granny turned to Bobby and said 'I think she is drunk, Bobby!' And sure enough, I was blind drunk. I had been at a party walking around and trying to amuse myself by grabbing and trying all the different kinds of drinks that people had left lying around. They had to take me to the hospital and get my stomach pumped it was that dangerous.

I think this paints an accurate picture of the overall father my father was to me!

This was not the only incident. As I was getting a bit older, I realized that there was something seriously wrong with my father. When you are a kid, you have this kind of innate feeling about what is going on with people, without actually really knowing any of the details. My father would take me shopping regularly; he was always 'buying' sheets and towels and things of that nature and then returning them almost immediately. I would watch him stealing sheets and towels and put them into different bags to return them. I knew deep down inside what he was doing was wrong. I was very young, but I didn't say anything. I just internalized a lot of the feelings that I had towards what was happening and my father in general and knew that I never wanted to be like him. These are the things that I remember, even today as an adult, they are the things that highlighted the path not to be taken, and they have moulded me into the person that I am today.

This story pre-frames and sets up why my values are so strong for honesty, integrity, family, commitment to your family, doing what you say at all times, and creating vows and sticking to them whether they are easy or not. My father didn't live that way. And from his teachings, I learned what not to do in life. Even though his lessons were hard and terrible, they are still valuable to me today.

I could sit here and make excuses for him, saying that it was his upbringing that made him the way he was and is, but that wouldn't be beneficial to anyone. People are who they choose to be, and my father wanted to be a roller coaster guy, living life to the extreme and on the edge at all times. It is not the way to live if you have a family, and although I like the rush of being on the edge too, I make sure that my family is always a priority and safe first.

I don't blame my father because everything happens for a reason and I know that everything we experience in life prepares us for that next person or event. For the life that we want to live, and then we can choose, we measure what is happening, and we can take the wrong side, and use that as leverage to turn it into good. I feel that my father's presence in my life was perfect. I also believe that everyone is put into our life for a reason, to frame us to wherever we want to go. Whether you call it the universe, God, a higher source, they put you in a position to help. We are co-creators of life. We impact everyone around us, whether, in a good way or a negative way, it doesn't matter because we have served our purpose and taught each other some lessons along the way.

I think that my father's part in my life helped co-create me into the *Unstoppable Momma* that I am today.

Just to cement the extreme unreliability of my father I will leave you with one more story. There was another occasion when I was about eight years old. Early in the morning, snow had just fallen for the very first time. I was at my father's house, and he had a huge dog named Bruno. Bruno was a Great Dane/St Bernard. He had a great big huge lion mane, and my father lived with this dog and five other people. One of those other people was my best friend and cousin, Jenny; she was my savior when I had to stay over at my father's house.

This house was more of a shack now that I think about it. A crash pad for the waifs and strays of life to come and sober up or get drunk depending on what day of the week it was or where the moon was sitting in regards to Saturn. It was early in the morning, and my father was still asleep, and my cousin Jenny and I were jumping up and down on the bed. All of a sudden the dog jumped up and bit me right on the face. The top teeth went through my left eye; his bottom teeth through my lower lip and chin. Bruno bit straight through my face to the point where my whole face flopped over.

As a side note, let me just clarify a few things. My dad and his sister married my Mom and her brother. So literally a brother and sister married another brother and sister. Jenny's life was very similar to mine, which is probably why we got along so well. Her mother turned into a prostitute drug addict, and my father was ... well, you get the picture of him. Thank goodness we had each other and stable parents who remarried and helped maintain the structure of our life. It allowed us to look and reflect on the things that we did not want to do in our lives. I tell you this part so that you know that my time spent with my father at his house would have been unbearable if it weren't for my soul sister Jenny.

Sure enough, I was yelling at my Dad to come and help me. Jenny was yelling hysterically too. He was sleeping because he had had a really late the night before, tons of people were always partying there, drinking until the wee hours of the morning, and the night before had been no different.

Once I had finally woken him up, he knew that it was bad, and he had to take me to the hospital but instead of just driving me right there, like a normal concerned father would, he took me to the 'old timers' bar that he often frequented. That is where we spent most of our time together. Because he had been up so late, he didn't want to drive me to the hospital and get in trouble from the police or doctors for being under the influence. So he took me to the bar, with a rag on my face and asked someone else to take me to the hospital. I remember thinking to myself 'Why am I sitting here? Why haven't we rushed to the hospital?' My parents arrived and my Dad, Mom had remarried by this stage, wanted to kill my father. And who can blame him? Left in his care, I was now mutilated with half my face hanging off. All because of his own selfish desire to drink and party until the wee hours of the morning.

Although my Mom did her best, to do the right thing by my father and me, she wanted him to see me and for me to see him. She never wanted me to feel abandoned by him or have me think that she kept him from me. Although I don't believe she realized the harm that there was at his place, or she would never have let me go.

There was another time I remember when my father driving down the street, I was about 5 and back in those days you didn't have to wear seatbelts, so no one did. He was driving a truck and jamming to The Stones. *"I'm so hot for her ...'* I remember the song well, jamming and him with his front teeth over his bottom lip, and he was smoking a joint. Even though I was a kid, I knew what was going on; I knew it was wrong.

He started talking to me, all the while jamming to the song. When all of a sudden he smashed into the back of another car. I smashed into the dashboard of his car. He stopped, he got out, checked on the people in the other car, then finally came over to see if I was okay. I was like 'Dad I think I am bleeding'. Blood was rushing down my face. What was the first thing he did? Yep, he took me back to the 'old timers' bar. Because he had just smoked a joint and knew that he couldn't go to the hospital having substances in his body. It is utterly ridiculous if you stop and think about all of these incidents in one sitting.

So this is the way that I grew up in the very beginning of my life. It was really tough, but I only know that retrospectively. At the time it was just my reality. Even though I knew there was something 'off' about the way my father behaved, he was my father so no matter how disappointed I was in him I loved him anyway. And I didn't know anything different, so I just went with it.

Like I said earlier, I don't blame anyone for the things my Mom and father did. In fact, it is just the opposite, from a very young age I had an excellent grounding in what I didn't want my life to turn out like.

2

Brian's Childhood

Life is made up of decisions. Even indecision is a decision that you make. If you choose not to make a decision, then you stay stagnant so in effect, you have made the decision to do nothing. I am going to introduce you to myself and my life as a member of the Unstoppable Family by highlighting for you some of the decisions that I have made in my life that have led me to this very point today.

I grew up in a small town called Cambridge Illinois, in the Midwest USA. Out of 2000 people 31 graduated from my high school class. My Grandfather created the first variety store, megastore in the world. Everybody knows of Walmart, Kmart, Target. They have essentially been modelled off what grandfather built Swan and Bosons, early in the mid-1900's. My father and my mom were divorced when I was five or six years old, and my father was actually gay.

My father died of aids. When I was eleven years old, we knew something was wrong. We never talked about it though before my father died. But he did contract aids back in the day when no one knew what it was. Which is probably why we never talked about it. There wasn't any language to use that helped us understand what was happening to my father, so we just left everything unsaid. It may not have been the right way to handle the situation back then, but there just wasn't a good way to tell us that our father had a death sentence, and there was nothing anyone could do about it. So we just never said anything.

That was the biggest thing and the most pivotal part of my life. He knew he was sick; he was aware that he had an expiration date, but he didn't know when it was. He actually wasn't sure he was going to be living, one month, three months, six months, one year, two years, five years. Fortunately, he was able to live for five years with the disease, and remained pretty healthy throughout, until the very end. He passed away when I was 16 years old, just two weeks before my seventeenth birthday and it was devastating. Even though I knew, to some degree that it was always going to end up that way, it killed me to know that he was gone. I think what may have hurt more was that he knew, and he never talked about this with me or any of his kids. I believe he was trying to protect us, or he just didn't know how to tell us that he was dying. But I was so unprepared for it that it took me a really long time to feel anything again.

His whole life switched from the moment he found out that he was sick. He was an entrepreneur and a very busy man all of the time, but once he found out that he was sick he basically just halted and started to go and see the world. The best way I can give an analogy on it is if you have seen 'The Bucket List.' My father actually lived the bucket list before it came out in the movies.

He took us, kids, I have a brother, Todd, who is four years older than me, my sister, Kim, is seven years older than me. He just took us traveling all around the world. He was trying to pack as much living into a short amount of time as possible. The first trip I took with him, it was the first time I was ever on a plane, was when I was 12 years old, we went to the UK and Amsterdam.

The following year we went to Greece. Then we took a couple of trips with everyone, my brother, sister and my Dad and I went to Hawaii. My brother and my sister and I went to Egypt when I was sixteen. We actually took a Caribbean cruise which was just five months before he passed away. That was in January of 1991. So you can see that he really tried to live a life with us before he died. He was packing our life full of memories with him so that when he did pass we would always have these wonderful trips to look back on. I don't know if that made it easier or harder at the time, but I am thankful now that I have all of those memories with him, my brother and my sister.

There were a couple of the main things in my life that really switched within me. When this small little town found out that my father was gay it was at a pivotal point in my brother's life, he was fifteen, I was eleven at the time, and my sister was eighteen. It was a colossal point of his life, and it was a time where people just shunned him. He felt so out of touch with people that he actually turned into a druggie, and so did my sister. They were the smokers. They used to be athletes, but they turned from it because of ridicule and people not wanting to interact with them. They retreated into their own little world where no one could touch them or hurt them. I was young enough where it didn't really affect me like it did Todd and Kim. When they turned that way I was thinking 'why are they doing that?' My brother even went to drug rehab when he was fifteen years old. It is funny how and why things happen to certain people at certain points in their life.

I remember, one day, sitting in Mr Stall's class, it was a biology class, my freshman year, I was just an average student (B's and C's) nothing great, just in the middle. But in that class I made a decision, I was just looking up and out of the window, and I said 'You know what, I'm going to be the best athlete in my class. I am going to be the best student in my class.' I remember sitting there making that decision, and once I made that decision I thought 'What do I have to do?' Everything that I have done in my life has led me to the person that I am today. Without each and every event and decision in my life, I would be a completely different person.

I started studying 15 minutes extra per night, nothing huge, but it was something. I was an average kid, but I did not become the number 1 kid in my class, I was just slightly behind Becky Swiger, I was number 2. But I gave a speech when I graduated. For athletics, I was just kind of in the middle of the road, just a little above average. I was very skinny; I don't even think I reached 100 pounds. Not really skilled. When I made that decision, I turned to a couple of people that I looked up to, that were just one year younger than my brother, and they were just lifting weights, and they were great athletes. I wanted to be like them, they were also wild and fun. I thought 'man I want to be like those guys.'

So I started pumping iron with them and lo and behold I went from just an average kid playing one side of the offense or defence of football to playing both sides, becoming all conference, I was the best athlete. So I did become the best athlete and almost the top student during my time at high school. That was one of the biggest things I achieved and one of the biggest moments in my life. I would have just kept on going if I hadn't have made that decision way back then. I would have continued to be that average student.

My father passed away while I was in my junior year, which would be year 11, two weeks before my seventeenth birthday. It was at that point where I thought life was going to be different. Nothing really happened beyond.

3

My Dad, As Opposed To My Father!

My Mom remarried a man that I have always thought of like my Dad, and have always called Dad. He was more of a father to me than my father. Therefore, I believe he deserves the respect and title of 'Dad' in my life. My Dad was a very strict and controlling man. I can't really blame him, he was taking on a woman with a shady past and 5 year old daughter, so it was a big undertaking to embark upon. I never knew why he was so strict and mean when I was a little girl; the truth didn't come to me until much later in life. Well I guess he was not mean to me, just very rigid in his approach to life. I actually quite liked the predictability of him and the rules that he imposed on our house. It gave me a sense of security that I had never felt before.

Some of Dad's family secrets and history started to reveal themselves to the world the longer we all lived together. Like the fact that his Mom was physically challenged, and his dad had one leg shorter than the other, and that he had had polio when my dad was a little boy. Having one leg shorter than the other was hard on my Dad's Dad, he had what they call 'little man syndrome,' and he embodied the phrase as we know it today. Because of his condition, he did not respect women what so ever, and because he was physically challenged he felt that he had something to prove to the world, he wanted to exert his dominance over women. The information came to my Mom and myself in little-filtered packets of information and by the time I was a teenager I had pieced together that my Dad's Dad had actually sexually abused his daughters because he had grown to hate women so much.

My Dad's mom had multiple sclerosis and couldn't walk and yet she had raised eight children and somehow pulled through without hurting any of them or resorting to violence. No one really knew the extent of what had happened until my Dad's sisters started to speak out about what had been happening. My Aunt Katie was one of them, we all thought she was a little slow in some way because she was a bit of a recluse, but we came to realize that she was just hiding from the world because she was so ashamed of what happened to her in the past.

Once my Dad's Mother found out what was happening, she packed up the kids and left. His Dad refused to let one of his oldest daughter go and kept her there. He eventually married her, and they had children together. I can't even imagine how her life would have been.

My dad was walking into a life, with this as his past. My mother a naive your girl, an ex-husband drug addict, crazy man, an Indian father in law and a southern mother in law and a 5 year old little girl. It was no wonder that he was strict and a bit standoffish around me. But my Paw Paw loved him. He knew that he was a strong, reliable guy and a good man for my mother and me. He was a firefighter after all, and my Mom knew that he would take care of us.

He walked into a relationship with my mother and was afraid even to touch me. I didn't know any of the backstories then, so I wasn't sure why he was so strict all of the time. But I knew, even then, that he had been brought into my life for a reason and I was grateful to him for the stability that he provided.

He really took over our family. I was removed from the unstructured chaos that my life had been for the last five years, into a new stable, if a little unaffectionate life. I was no longer sleeping in different places, or moving around all of the time. And best of all I was able to be part of their wedding. They really included me in all of their life and decisions.

My Dad's favorite statement was 'If you're going to do something you don't do it half-assed. Do it right the first time. Don't waste people's time. Live with pure integrity of what you believe in.' These are the lessons that I have learned from my Dad, and they were all the clearer because they were in total contrast to everything that I had learned for the first five years of my life.

So there I was living in the all-American lifestyle with my all-American family. From the outside to people who didn't know our back story, we looked like the idyllic American family. My Dad the firefighter, my Mom the stay at home Mom and me the perfect little only child growing up with two loving parents.

I was so proud of my Dad, and I would tell anyone that would listen that my Dad was a hero because he was a firefighter. He would leave early in the morning and not return until the next morning. Now that I think of it, he had such a dangerous job. I would smell the fire on his clothes when he came home in the morning from fighting fires and saving lives all night. We lived in Detroit, that says it all. It wasn't easy for my Mom to always be home with me alone, but I was so happy that I finally had someone that I could look up to and think of as a role model in my life. I remember when I was young we only had 1 car, so my Mom would drive my Dad to work early in the morning, and I would lay in the back of the van with blankets. It was a fun adventure when we would chase the fires, but now that I think about it, that was seriously dangerous. Although my Dad was strict, he was strict because he cared so much. He raised me to be bold and vigorous. He said 'You never start a fight, but you should always finish it!' That was the kind of man that he was and still is.

He was the one that got me into playing softball. He would whip a softball as fast as he could at me and I thought it was just horrible. But I loved it at the same time. I loved being pushed beyond what I thought my limits were. I loved being forced into uncertain circumstances and being made to feel uncomfortable for a few moments. Because when you have someone who will support you through it all and makes you feel good about yourself, you can reach incredible limits that you never thought were possible.

He pushed me, and pushed me and that is how I became a great softball player. I dove into the sport. I am a Gemini; I have always known and thought about the addictive side of my personality. So I realized that if I was going to have an addictive personality, I better make sure that it is addicted to something healthy and beneficial to my future. I wasn't into drinking, I wasn't into raving and partying. I was into being the best, and I chose to be the best softball player there was.

I studied peak performance and learned everything there was about it. I started to play softball in high school then I met one of the best coaches around. Coach Callahan who really supported me in my athletic adventure. She became my mentor. She brought me into a national softball team tryout, playing for a travel team. I got picked up, and they taught me how to be an even better player, and they turned me into a left-hand hitter as well. I just became very skilled at the sport and put everything I had into it. I was so fast, and they taught me how to be a base stealer, they made me into the player that I had always wanted to be.

All the way through high school I was running track and field and training incredibly hard at softball. Before I knew it, it was time to go to college. I started to look into colleges that I wanted to go to and didn't put any limits on myself other than striving for greatness. Although my family was very supportive of me going to college and making my own future, they still had a poverty mindset about their aspirations and life ambitions. But I never had that mindset and pushed myself to do whatever I wanted. I went to try out for U of M and Florida State. Both of which are Division One schools.

I was accepted to both schools.

However, I was only offered to be a "Red Shirt" opportunity for the first year. Meaning, you go to school for that first year and pay upfront, and then over the next four years you play softball (or another sport that you excel at), and your schooling is paid for.

The strength of my Dad and the support and confidence that he had in me made him say 'No way; she is going to play for you, and you need to pay from the beginning.' But that's not how it works in Division one schools, and my Dad didn't think we should pay. It was fiercely competitive, so I didn't get to go to either of those schools. Instead, I went to a Division Two school that ended up paying for all of the years that I studied there. It was a private business school, and they had a good softball program with an intense coach. So I was extremely happy to be part of their community.

Even though I was really upset that I didn't get to attend my first choice college, everything happens for a reason and if I had ended up going to one of those schools my life may have taken a different path. I finished my career in softball during university but I stayed and played for the US women's national team. I not only played but had the opportunity to coach throughout Europe. As a player, our team won 4 gold medals and this was before the Women's US Olympic team was on the scene. I started to feel as though my life was really developing, I was becoming an athlete and using my past experiences with addiction and chaos to really forge my own path and make a life for myself.

I was a high-end athlete, was addicted to playing sport, and so in the offseason I had an abundance of energy that needed a positive outlet. So I started to do bodybuilding. And along with the bodybuilding, I became really addicted to body image and how I looked. I worked in a gym and taught aerobics so I had an amazing body, but with that there comes this expectation that you can maintain it at all times.

So there I was a young woman in college with a promising future. I was heavily into sports, softball, and bodybuilding, but I couldn't let my guard down even for one second because I had built this image around myself. I could have transitioned into the fitness and nutrition side of things at school or even gone out and found myself a mentor. But instead, I just became my mentor. I would read books and constantly try to learn new things about fitness and nutrition. I always had a good guide who would push me in the right direction, but I never had someone that I could look up to and really get guidance from in an experienced tone.

When I think about it, I have always been my own mentor. What I have now learned though is that without a mentor you can't go to that next level, you are always just one step ahead of your body in your head, and if you really want to succeed you need to be pushed by someone who is 5 or 6 steps in front of you. You can only know what you know, so you can't take what you teach yourself from a book and keep thriving and succeeding because you don't even know what to aspire to. The same is true in business.

I was winning awards and receiving accolades for my success, and it felt great. I was at peak performance and loving every minute of it. I was perfect; I looked perfect there was nothing that I would have changed about my life at that moment. But then I started to realize that other people thought that I was perfect too. I would hear people say 'Oh Rhonda would never eat that cookie, she wouldn't order pizza for lunch!' And I started to feel this outside pressure to look and be perfect all the time. It was at that moment that I began to build my whole life based on what other people thought I should do.

I really began to focus on how I looked. I wouldn't say that it led to feelings of low self-confidence, but it was low self-esteem. I was always trying to be better than what everyone thought I was. But deep down inside I just really wanted to eat fucking pizza!

It got to the point where I would only eat when I was by myself; I would scoff pizza and ice cream until I couldn't breathe and then when I didn't want it in my stomach anymore more I would go and make myself throw up. I carried on this way from about the age of 20 to 27 years old. Later in life, I learned that it was actually called bulimia and it is a severe condition. I wasn't living for me anymore, it was not the life that I wanted to lead so I found different ways to control it or manipulate it, and some of those ways were harmful to me.

I think many people fall into this trap as they are growing or developing. Some are at the very bottom of the rung, and some at the very top. For me, I always had to be the best. I would never allow myself to be less than the best. So I put a lot of pressure on myself. Many people fall into this rut. They either stay in the bottom because they feel as though they can never achieve, so they don't try. Or they are at the very top, and you can never go any lower, you have to work super hard to stay at the top all of the time because anything less would be like losing.

It is such an important and valuable lesson for growing adults, business owners and parents to understand, that being in a rut is only escapable by your own hand. You have to ask yourself 'Who am I?', 'What do I believe in?' You have to be true to yourself. Stop caring what other people think of you and live for yourself, that is how you get out of a rut. It wasn't until I was in my late 20's, and after I had married my husband that I really stopped caring what other people thought about me.

Success is nothing more
than a few simple disciplines,
practiced every day.
Jim Rohn

4

The Big Move

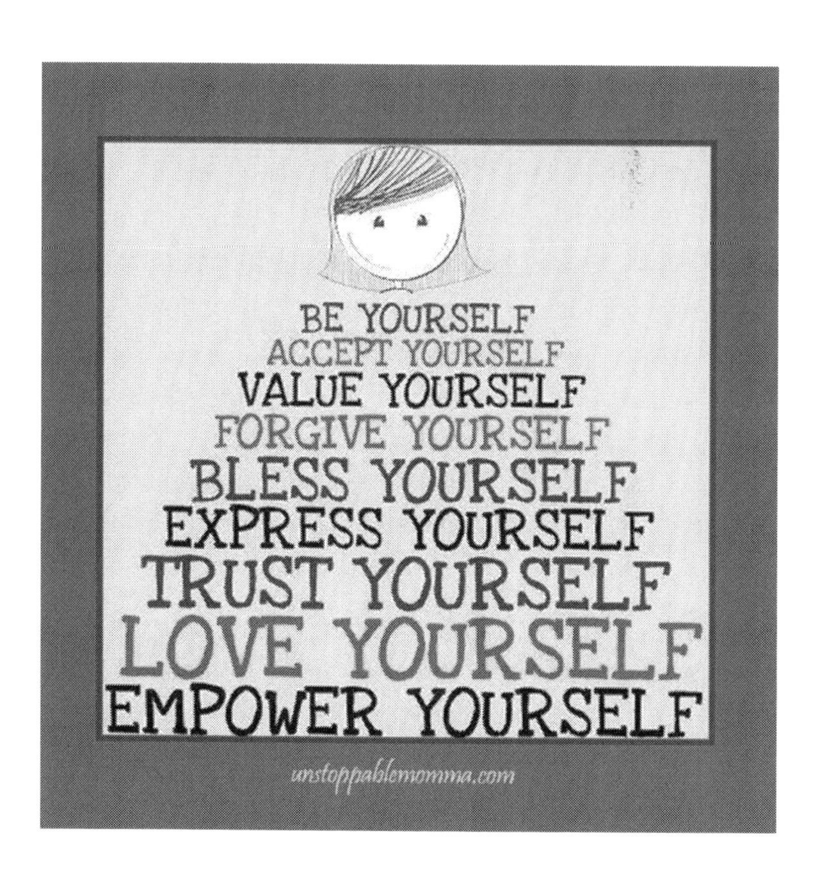

Once I was finished with the undergraduate part of my degree I decided that I would stay on and go to graduate school and complete my Master's. I stayed for an extra 15 months and during that time I studied and coached softball.

I always knew that I wanted to leave my family and strike out on my own. Although I loved them dearly and with all my heart they were different to the person that I had become and wanted to keep moving towards. They definitely had a different mindset and were very rigid in their approach to life and choices. I knew that I needed to surround myself with different people if I wanted to reach the aspirations that I had set for myself.

I needed to get away. I had always said to my Mom that my heart belonged in California so when I finished my Master's degree I went looking for jobs in California. I was hired by Philip Morris and they said to me 'We will hire you in Michigan and transfer you to California in a year." I thought to myself there is no way I am ever getting to California if I just do what they say. I knew that there would be excuse after excuse about why they needed me to stay in Michigan, it is just the nature of business.

So I took matters into my own hands and called the California office and told them that I had been hired in Michigan but I wanted to be in California, and they hired me right then and there over the phone, flew me out to California for an interview to seal the deal. It really pissed the Michigan office off but I just told them that if they really cared about the company it shouldn't matter to them where I was stationed just that their company was getting the best possible candidate for the job. Philip Morris, California, flew me out there and I checked out San Diego and San Francisco. I chose San Diego as my spot to start my new life.

I absolutely fell in love with the freedom or having my own job, my own house and no one around me having any kind of expectation about how I should live my life. I was in a completely new place where no one knew me at all. I could be whoever I wanted to be. I didn't have to be the survivor of a crazy drug addict father, or the little girl of a hero firefighter, or even the softball player/ bodybuilder that everyone looked to for inspiration. I was just me, I was Rhonda for the first time in a very long time. I went to California with a whole new vision, passion and zest for life, I was ready to begin to lead my perfect life and to create whatever I wanted to get out of it.

One of the perks of my new job was that I had the freedom to go into the office whenever I wanted, because I was employed into the outside sales department. True to California style I fell in love with surfing, I lived extremely close to the beach and decided that as part of my new zest and passion for a perfect life I would start my day with a trip to the beach every morning. The first day that I headed down there, I could see these guys surfing and having fun and so I decided that I was going to learn how to surf. It was going to be my new thing.

Along the beaches in California there are places where you can rent a surfboard about every 25 meters, so I went and rented a foam board from one of the places that offer this service.

Along the beaches in California there are places where you can rent a surfboard about every 25 meters, so I went and rented a foam board from one of the places that offer this service.

I walked up to them and said, "I'm going to learn to surf," and they were like, "Okay. You are seeing some of the biggest swells of the year right now, the biggest." It was an El Nino year in San Diego, in 1998. "You need to be careful, only go to these small places that I am marking on the map for you, otherwise you will get into trouble." And I was like, "Yeah, yeah, whatever." Do you not realize that I am an athlete, I can do anything I set my mind to. I am beginning my perfect life over here. So I went to one of the biggest spots, in La Jolla Shores, and I got out there I realized it was massive. I didn't realize that it was going to be dangerous. I just thought that I was a strong swimmer and I had a floating device with me, there would be no problem at all.

As I paddled out there I remember thinking to myself "Oh my God, I feel like I am going to die." There was one big crashing wall of water after the other and I had no idea how to get out of there. I was trying to figure out how the hell I was going to get back to shore and I am sure that I looked like the perfect tourist idiot, or a deer caught in headlights. All of a sudden I hear this voice from above the waves yelling at me "You have to paddle that way if you want to get back in." And I thought to myself "Oh thank God my savior has come to rescue me." Little did I know.

I finally got back into shore I was exhausted but totally exhilarated at the same time. It was my new addiction. I didn't have to be the softball extraordinaire, or the bodybuilder that everyone aspired to be like, I just had to be me and do things that I loved and felt passionate about. I wanted to take care of my body still and eat well but I also wanted to be able to have fun and play while I did it.

I took a rental board from the guy at the surf shop and he charged me $10 a day, I ended up accidentally keeping for 2 months. If you do the maths correctly, you will realize that it cost me $600 to rent a board that would have cost just over $800 to buy brand new. When I went to return the board he ended up only charging me $500 for the two months but told me flat out that I needed to buy my own board.

I went out searching for the perfect board and while I was shopping I decided that the six miles that I lived from the beach was far too far away. There is that addictive personality thing creeping back in. I knew that I needed to live on the beach, not next to the beach but actually on it. I needed to be surrounded by it. Feel it in my soul. This is the hustle part. I found a little apartment on the bay side of mission beach, in my heart I knew that by visualizing and being determined to do something, you know you can achieve it. You focus on what you want and write it down, and tell yourself every day that you can do it. That you are going to do every single thing in your power to achieve your dream no matter what. I had laser beam focus, I went for it and did everything in my power to ensure that I achieved it.

I was loving my new life in my new apartment right across the beach, and I paddled out to surf every day and teach myself the basics of surfing and beach life. I was in love with the atmosphere. In San Diego I lived in Mission Beach and there is a long stretched out boardwalk which is just awesome. There is everything from roller skaters to dog walkers, to runners and bike riders. It is California living at it's finest. I would walk across the street to the boardwalk every morning, and there was this one group of people that I had to pass every day that just sat there and smoked and drank and partied. I was still in the trained athlete mode of living, I didn't drink, smoke and I was vegetarian, so I avoided them like the plague because I knew with my personality there are only extreme behaviors. I either don't participate or I out party everyone! At this time, I was only trying to focus on myself and my happiness so I didn't want to be seduced by this lifestyle that I could easily fall into. When you are not structured or controlled about your decisions you can fall off the path that you have chosen for yourself and be seduced by an easier path.

After a little while I start to notice that this one guy is always surfing at the same time as me, getting closer and closer to where I am waiting for the perfect wave. He had sandy blonde hair, and from the way he spoke to me I could tell he was from the Midwest. He wasn't Californian but he surfed, which made him just like me and someone that I felt connected too, but he was a bit annoying, rambunctious and wild, really goofy and funny, and he was always around. I saw him at the beach with the same group of people all the time.

After a couple of weeks of paddling around me in the surf he finally worked up enough courage to talk. He said, 'Hey, you from around here?' I was pretty standoffish with my reply because I thought his first attempt at conversation was pretty lame. I mean I had seen him here every day for the previous couple of weeks, so of course he knew that I am from around here. I just thought to myself, 'Whatever, idiot!' That is just my nature, but this guy just kept on chatting, like he didn't get the hint that I was a bitch. He persisted and eventually introduced me to some of his surfing buddies. We all became really good friends and I was so excited and happy that I had my own little surfing crew to hang out with.

We started to hang out more and more and he became my buddy. We even started going to the gym together, I eventually got over his idiocy and incessant talking. After one gym session he turned to me and said "Hey, let's go get some food.' I thought we just spent all of that time in the gym and now you want to go and eat? But I didn't want to let my old insecurities about eating come back into my life. This guy didn't know the lengths that I used to go to to maintain my body, so I wasn't about to let him see me be weird around food. We went to a place called Saska's, it is a Sushi restaurant with a top deck, just off Mission Boulevard, it was the fancier spot in mission.

Although we both had corporate jobs at the time, I was working for Philip Morris and he was a robotics engineer, we weren't really into spending a lot of money, we preferred to spend money on things that mattered - like living on the beach and surfboards!

We walked into the restaurant and he decided that we were

going to eat our sushi on the top deck, which was closed. He walked up to a waitress and told her something that was just out of earshot of me and sure enough she opened up the barrier for us to be able to go to the top deck. As we sat there eating and chatting over our sushi, I thought to myself 'Are we on date? Yes, this is a date! I have actually accidentally fallen into a date with this guy!'

We hid our relationship for several months. I moved in with 2 of our surf buddies, Rolf and Paul on the boardwalk right next door. After a few months everyone figured it out and we quickly started dating regularly after this and it was the pure dating life of two surfer dudes. We lived next door to each other at the beach and we surfed together every day, then we both went off to corporate jobs that kept us in the lifestyle that we wanted to live. We had amazing surfing buddies and we all lived at the beach. I just remember thinking to myself throughout this time - 'I have finally made it!'

I am not saying that I was rich or becoming a powerhouse in the sales industry. But I felt like I had made it because I was finally being myself. That meant more to me than anything else on earth. I had the ability to really explore who I was and what I wanted out of life. And for the first time ever I was able to act like myself without pressure from anyone around me. I was living the dream.

5

Brian - Here's Another Big Decision In My Life

"Don't wish it was easier, wish you were better.

Don't wish for less problems, wish for more skills.

Don't wish for less challenge, wish for more wisdom."

Jim Rohn

I was a senior in high school, so my last year, when I went to my guidance counselor to map out what I wanted to do after high school. I sat down with Mr Mungerson, and he asked me 'What do you want to do?' and I told him 'I really don't know.' He asked me 'what are you really good at?' and I said 'I am good at maths and science.' And he said 'Do you know that engineers make the most, coming out of university, coming out of college, right off the bat?' So I said, 'Really, that sounds like something I want to do.' So right there in that 5-minute conversation, I made a decision that dictated the next 14 years of my life. Then I had to pick which university I wanted to go to. My brother was going to a state school that pretty much anybody could get into. If you had a pulse and you could put the money on the table, you could get into it. It was a fun party school. I could have gone there and spent one or two years with my brother, and it would have been fantastic. But then I made another decision. I thought 'If I am going to make the decision to become an engineer, why wouldn't I go to the best school that I could?'

While I was at the University of Illinois, I joined a fraternity. It was amazing, and I had the best time of my life. Coming from a small town with 31 people in your graduating class and 2000 people in your town to going to an undergrad school with 40,000 people. I had more people in my dorm room, in my square block, that were my own age versus my whole town. My life was just completely different.

I was like 'Holy Cow, this is as fun as possible.' So I joined a fraternity, which is big in the United States and I had incredible friends. It was the time in my life. Engineering was the most difficult thing I had ever done. I went from hardly doing any study in high school, just enough to get a few A's to being with the world's best, and top students in my classes. I had to study non-stop. But I thought it was worth it. I never watched TV, I just studied. Monday through Thursday I studied then Friday, Saturday, and Sunday, I partied.

So I was living the university and American lifestyle, and in my second year of university, I got this itch. I thought this is great, I love the university, but there has to be something else. I kept noticing wherever I went a thing about student exchange. I remember talking to my friends and fraternity about studying abroad. They said to me 'Are you friggin crazy? You are going to give up a year of the best parties and chicks to study abroad?' I knew there was something else out there for me and I wanted to check it out.

I was so naive, and I didn't really know a whole lot. I thought that there were only three countries that spoke English, the UK, Australia and the United States, which is embarrassing but true. So I thought 'Where do I go? Should I go to the UK or should I go to Australia?' I wanted something different, so I picked sunny Australia. I always had this fascination with surfing, so Australia was very appealing to me. I remember when I was 6 or 7 years old, and we got cable TV and I would watch Surfer Magazine, even though we were miles away from an ocean. So I decided that I needed to go to Australia and do the surfer thing.

I made the decision to go to Perth's Curtin University in WA, and I lived there from 1994 to 1995.

The very first night I was in Perth I met up with a whole bunch of girls and we partied. They were so fascinated by me being American, I thought the rest of the world hated Americans, but not in Australia; they loved me. My last name being Swan helped as well because Perth is all about swans, 'Swan River,' 'Swan Brewery', so I was very well liked in Perth. The girls wanted to show me around their city and asked me where I wanted to go, do and see. I wanted to go to the beach, which we did, had a few beers and then I was faced with another big decision.

We were at Cottesloe Beach, I saw a hot chick in a bikini and in the distance and I saw a surfer get barrelled. I went 'Holy Cow, SOLD.' This was going to be my lifestyle forever. That was back in '94, I had never surfed before and now, 22 years later, and I am the ***Unstoppable Surfer*** dude. I went and got a surfboard, which by the way was the hardest board to learn on, but I kept persisting. I actually bought a short board; everyone told me to buy a longboard because it would get me up and going, but I didn't listen. So I learned the hard, and it took me longer to actually surf. But it was something that I really wanted, so I kept at it.

By the time I left Australia, I could stand up on a board, but I was definitely still a novice. I was hooked on surfing. I had one of the best years of my life.

The difference between being at Curtin University compared to the University of Illinois was that they did not load you up as much in Australia so I only had to study about 25% as much as I did back home to get the same grades. I could have about 25% as much as I did back home to get the same grades. I could have used the time to improve my grades but i was still B student, and now a novice surfer. It's all about decisions.

I was there for a year, and I travelled all around Australia. That is where my travel bug came from. I went to Bali Indonesia, which is where I am right now. The more I travelled the more I realized, this is a big world. I was blown away by Bali, Indonesia. And I thought 'how can I live here?' It wasn't possible at the time because there was nothing for me to do there. But that was one of the things that I had in my mind. On the way home I went to New Zealand and took an RV from the South Island and up through the North Island and did the whole camper van thing. I thought New Zealand was the best, and that it had the most beautiful country surrounds in the world. Then I went to Fiji and Hawaii and when I came back to the University of Illinois and was back with my friends I was a totally different person.

At first I was so excited to tell everybody what I had done, they would pretend to listen and then it was straight back to the fraternity and university lifestyle and party. My buddy, who had joined me for 6 months, was trying to tell everybody about his experience, and nobody wanted to listen to him either. Nobody wanted to hear about it. I thought it was very interesting. Then something just clicked with me. People are in a matrix, and I was just a different person.

After my travels I felt like a completely different person. I decided I that was going to finish my engineering degree. I wanted to be a surfer, but I had to finish my degree first. 90% of the people that go to the University of Illinois are from Chicago or the suburbs, and after they finish their degree, they move back and work in Chicago. It is just routine; that is what everybody did. I was like I am not going to do that. I thought I am a surfer. People thought I was crazy and I probably was at the time, but I knew what I wanted and I had to go for it. I kept watching this movie called 'The endless summer' I knew that was what I wanted to do. Even though it took me another year and a half to graduate, during which time I couldn't surf at all, I knew that it was what I wanted to do.

I started to interview for different jobs. At universities in America, companies come to the university and you do your interviewing right on campus. Since our school, for engineering, is prestigious, all of the good companies came to see us. You are almost guaranteed a job. I was interviewing and interviewing. One company called Parker Hannifin were based out of Northern California, and as I got a couple of job offers I decided to go with them as they were in California.

This is a year after I returned from Australia, where I had heard so many stories about Australians traveling around America, which I had never done. I realized that when you live in a country you tend not to see your own place, just as I had seen a lot of Australia and NZ, which my Aussie friends hadn't. We get into a mindset of I'll do that someday. So now I had to decide if I was going to get an internship, like

95% of my fellow classmates or go and travel around the USA.

By now I had really developed the travel bug and so I went traveling from Florida all throughout the southwest, came back to Illinois, did the drive out to Mount Rushmore. I bought a National Park Pass because the United States has incredible National Parks. I just went traveling in my '81 Firebird for three months. I went to all these National parks all the way down to Baja California to Utah, up through Oregon, Washington, Mt Saint Helens, Arizona for the Grand Canyon. I saw everything in the United States; then I went on tour with Phish, and then I came back did the responsible thing and graduated from University.

Now I had one semester left in college before I graduated. I accepted my job and moved out to Northern California. I was a sales engineer, for Parker Hannifin. I was going to be in Northern California for six months. When I moved to California, I was like Holy Cow; this is frigging awesome. It was just north of San Francisco. I got to hang out in the city, and I had money coming in because I had a job and no expenses. All of my friends were back in Chicago, Illinois and I was out there by myself in California, I was a freak once again. I was in love with it. It was amazing.

So I got a surfboard and started surfing again. After 3-4 months into my new position the company started to position their graduates around the United States where they needed territory managers. As they knew I was from Chicago they offered me a great job in a great location in nearby Wisconsin. I said 'No.' And nobody said 'no' when they handed something out to you and said this it, you took it and didn't have a choice. I thought about it for a while and came back to them a couple of days later and said "I appreciate the offer, it is going to be a good territory, it is where my family is, but I am a surfer. I love California, and I want to be here.' And they told me there was nothing open in California. We went back and forth for a week or two and people started to move to their new positions. And I said 'I know it costs a lot to hire me and I love this job, but here is what is going to happen, I am going to get there and I am going to get the bug of 'I can't be here' and then I will probably quit.' I told them flat out, not knowing if I was going to get fired for that.

I said if you want I can continue to work here in the office until something opens up. I worked there longer than everybody else. I thought it was cool because I had all my expenses paid while I was staying there. Finally, they were like, hey this person is going on maternity leave in Southern California. I wanted to stay in Northern California, but Southern California was a bit glitzier. I moved, it was in Orange County, I was in Newport Beach. I was once again, 'Holy Cow this is so friggin cool'. I started telling my friends, who were all still in Chicago, they all thought I was a freak.

I started working in Southern California and while I was there I lived in Newport Beach, but the longer I stayed the more territory opened up in San Diego, so I decided with the company to move down there. I was attracted to a place called Mission Beach, it is in San Diego, and it is a complete beach community. I was right at home there, it was the best thing I had done to date.

I got myself a one bedroomed apartment on the Mission Beach Boardwalk, and I instantly had hundreds of friends. Everybody lived on this one court called Jamaica Court, and it was like a melting pot of people from all around the United States. Newport Beach wasn't a melting pot, the people that lived there were born there and raised there and stayed there.

But San Diego was full of people who came from all over the world. There are hardly any natives there. They are a very rare breed, native San Diego's.

I was the kingpin living straight on the boardwalk. If you wanted to check the surf you had to sit in front of my house or my porch and party. There were people from New Orleans, New Jersey, Oregon, Florida, everywhere and we just became instant friends because nobody had any other friends with them, so we had to get along become each other's support and entertainment.

I moved there in January and in May I was out surfing in front of my house and that is when I saw Rhonda for the first time.

let's
just be
who we

6

Today I Met The Man I'm Going To Marry!

So okay not exactly the day I met the man I'm going to marry, but I love that song. And this was the time that we started to really get serious with each other and move our relationship to the next level. Brian and I had been dating for about 2 years when the lease was up on each of our houses. We decided that it was time to move in together, I had this shacky one bedroomed apartment right on the beach next door to all of our surfing buddies, so Rhonda moved in. It was a match made in heaven.

The house was so small that we actually had to build a loft to put our bed in and in order to get into bed every night we had to climb on the dresser and pull ourselves into bed. The apartment was really more of a beach shack but it was our beach shack and we loved it. But we were realists too and decided that it was probably about time that we started to invest money into property.

When Brian's Dad died he left his kids some money in order to ensure that they were able to set themselves and their families up for future success when and if they decided to settle down. Brian decided that this was his time to settle down and used the money so that we could invest in property and buy a house together to live in. We looked all over California for the right house for us to move into. And we finally found an amazing little two bedroomed ocean side home that had a top deck that overlooked the ocean. It was perfect for us.

A year later we were surfing at a beautiful remote beach on Christmas day and just enjoying life and having fun with each other. I decided to get out of the water a bit earlier than

Brian did, so I made my way back to the shore and realized that he was following me in. We had been together for three years at this time and never once had Brian left a good surf swell to follow me into shore. I thought something might be wrong. So I waited for him right on the beach where the water was lapping at my feet and just stood there trying to read his face. He looked like he was in pain and I started to get worried. As he reached the edge of the surf where I was standing, we both went to change into warm clothes. Came to the edge to enjoy the swell on Christmas Day and he fell to his knees and my heart jumped into my throat. I was thinking 'Oh my God what has happened out there for him to be on his knees?' I start to bend down towards him and just at that moment he lifts his head up and Mumbles 'Will you m-m-marry me?' It was the best mumble I had ever heard and I instantly said yes. Now my heart was in my throat for an entirely different reason.

He created this gorgeous ring. It was a trillion diamond, 3 point trillion diamond with waves. It was supposed to be the sun, the waves, and a surfboard, and it represented our connection in surfing. I realized at that very moment how well he actually knew me. He knew what I wanted out of life, he knew what I wanted to eat, he knew when I was angry for a reason, and when I was angry for no good reason, and with a little help from my bestie Lori, he knew what kind of ring I would love to wear for the rest of my life.

We decided that we would plan the wedding slowly because we were in no hurry, but our decision was to have it in Hanalei Bay, Hawaii. We were not in a rush in any way, shape or form and we were just enjoying life and having fun with each other. We also wanted to give everyone that we invited time to plan, organize, and save for such a big trip.

Hanalei Bay was gorgeous, we had been there to surf one year and had absolutely fallen in love with. The wedding itself was beautiful. We had 60 people attend and we got married on the waterfront at the Hanalei Colony Resort, it was the most magical moment of my life. We had flame throwers and Hula dancers and I had even learned how to the Hawaiian wedding song hula for Brian. That night as we were lying in bed together we decided that if we ever had a child we were going to call them Hanalei because it was place where dreams come true.

Sun & Surf, What More Can A Man Want

I was surfing at 6 am before work on a weekday. It was May of 1998, and I was surfing right in front of my house. 60 to 70 meters off shore and from a quart over, just a block. This hot chick with a big long board underneath her arm came over. We all wore wetsuits, but not her, she had a bikini bottom on with a rash top. She walked right passed my house, and I was like 'Whoa check out this chick!' About three doors down she knocked on the door and a dude came out, and I was like 'Argh she has a boyfriend.' They came paddling out, right by me, and I thought 'whatever, I am going to introduce myself.' So I said 'Hey I am Brian. Where are you from?' She said 'Santa Barbara' and I said 'That's a long drive for you to come here, and she said 'I live on Santa Barbara court' which is the court right next to me. I chatted her up a little bit, but that was about it. I saw her surfing every day with the same dude, and so I thought 'Oh she has a boyfriend, no big deal.'

One Friday afternoon we were all sitting around having a few beers, getting rowdy and playing horseshoes when the 'boyfriend' of Rhonda was talking about having a surfing girlfriend and how much he wished he had one. I said 'I thought you were with Rhonda' and he said "Nah we are just friends.' So then I thought right I am going in for the kill. This was just before the 4th of July, which is our independence day. Then on July 7th I was like 'Hey, want to go and get Sushi?' And she was like 'Yeah sure.'

We rode our skateboards down the boardwalk to a place called Saska's and I had planned a very romantic evening. I tipped the waitress and had her open up the top floor so we could be outside under the night sky. We had sushi by candlelight and then watched the fireworks display. But the real fireworks happened when she took me back to her place!

We have been together ever since.

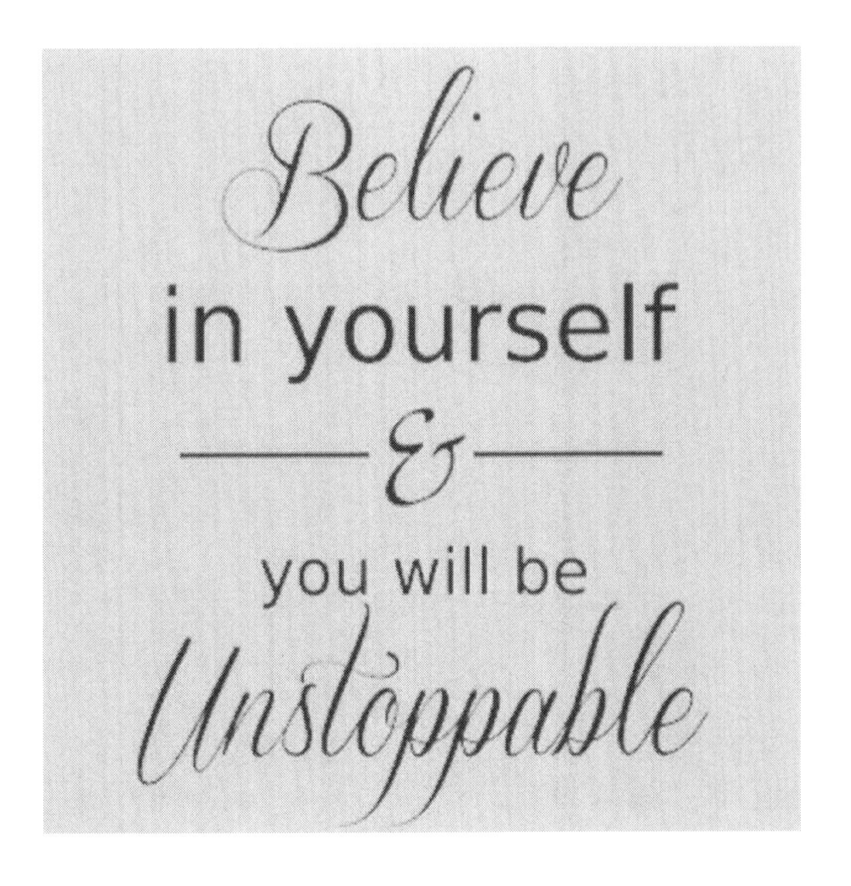
Believe
in yourself
&
you will be
Unstoppable

8

Decisions, Decisions, Decisions

"Our lives are a sum total of

the choices we have made."

Wayne Dyer

Our lives moved along as you would expect for a young married couple who were ambitious and in love with life. We were living in our beautiful house and moving up in the corporate world. I decided that I didn't want to work for Philip Morris any longer because the job wasn't offering me any stimulation. I loved a challenge, and still, do, and I just felt as though I wasn't working at my peak performance in that role.

Brian, however, is a little more relaxed than I am, he lives out loud and needs a lot of extra stimulation to keep him motivated and running at peak performance. He is a go-getter but nowhere near as extreme as I am. We balance each other out quite well, and this is a definite positive in a long term relationship. There is no denying that we were living the perfect existence, and Brian would have been happy to continue our lovely life and die a happy man. But I am always seeking more in life. I wanted a bigger house, more responsibility at work, more money, and a bigger family. So I started looking for different jobs and eventually got hired by GlaxoSmithKline pharmaceuticals. I was finally becoming the powerful corporate woman that I had always wanted to be.

I guess it stems from when I was a little girl. I never bought things or had them bought for me. So as I was going through college, I always envisioned and visualized myself being in a position where I could afford anything that I wanted. I visualized myself controlling a company because for a long time I didn't have any control over my life or my crazy parents, control was my ultimate goal.

While I was in the interview for my new pharmaceutical job, I met my mentor, the person that I knew could pull me to the next level of corporate living that I knew I wanted to achieve. She was perfect. Had the perfect power suit, perfect blonde bob with perfectly cut bangs, even her shoes were perfectly matched with her bag. I was sitting in the interview the whole time thinking to myself 'Oh my gosh this woman is the picture of perfection, I want to be like her in every way, and she is going to take me to the next level.' I felt so empowered just being the room with her, I stood up and started to sell them right away. I knew I had the job before the interview was even over. I knew that my life was about to move up to the next step.

Brian had a good job as well but he doesn't have that addictive drive to push to the next level like I do. I started thinking to myself that I had pushed him so far. I had forced him to get married; I was pushing the idea of kids, in general, I just continued to push next level stuff on him. I wanted all of this stuff, and he was just sitting back thinking 'Whoa, what's the deal here? Where is my life heading with this woman?'

In every relationship, there is one person that pushed you forward and another that helps you see the present. Brain helped me move forward in some aspects of my life, but he was also my balance. I have a perfectionist type personality so when I go for something it is at all cost. I push myself to the limit until I get what I want. Brian was there to balance me and make sure I enjoyed what was happening in our present instead of just looking to the future all of the time.

He allowed me to relax and just be me for a while. He didn't judge, and he didn't need more. I wanted more, and I had always wanted more. Not because I was unhappy with what I had but just because I couldn't stand to be static.

Finally, at the age of 25, I did start to relax a little bit, Brian had even got me loose enough to enjoy a party and couple of alcoholic drinks, on occasion. I wasn't wild or anything like that, but since I had been married to Brian, I had certainly given into my wilder side. He reigned me in and allowed me to be happy in all of the things that we had achieved up to this point, and I was able to push him forward to things he didn't even know he wanted.

We started to plan a future together, and we both realized that the best way for us to make money was to invest in property. We decided that we would take the money that we have earned from selling our last property and invest that into another house. So we had the money from our first home, and we decided to rent out our second home and remortgage it to buy a bigger more expensive house. It was a $1.4 million house that had just been built. It was completely awesome and made me feel as if we were walking up this perfect ladder. We were both intoxicated and overcome by it all to the point that when we were finally in the house, he just looked at me and said 'You're crazy!'

Everything moves along great for a little while until I start to get that feeling again that I want something bigger in my life. I begin to realize my age; I am 30 years old. I look at my surrounding; we live in a five bedroomed home. I look at my husband who I love more than anything in the whole world.

And it hits me. I want to start a family. That is my next something greater, something bigger. But at the same time, I realize that I can't be this big corporate woman and raise the family that I want to. Everything that I have worked up to this point starts to shift to the side as my new something bigger comes into focus. I ask myself some very deep questions that will change my future and my reality forever. Do I want to be a corporate woman, or do I want to raise a family?

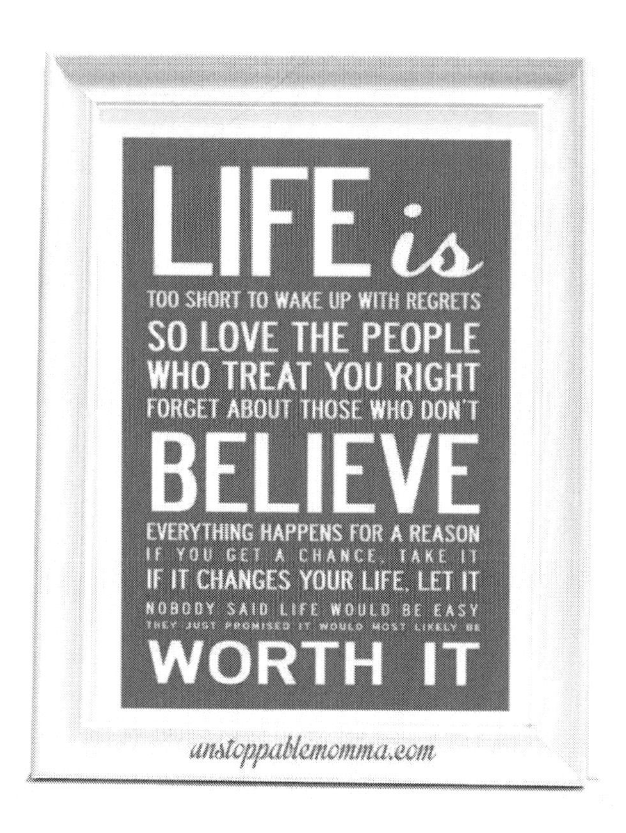

BELIEVE

The Wake-Up Call!

I have the perfect job at this point. I was running the western division pharmaceutical side in California. GlaxoSmithKline Pharmaceuticals. I got up each morning, and either ran on the beach or went for a surf. I'd get back home and shower, do my hair, maybe have a passing glance at my husband and then head off, in an hour of traffic, to my perfect job. Or so I thought until I had the wake-up call of a lifetime.

It was Monday morning, and I was sitting in the boardroom with my mentor and boss, Jane. Even though I had been working with Jane for a few weeks at this point, I was still in awe of her. She was perfect from her hair to her shoes; nothing was out of place. Jane started the meeting perfectly on time, like everything else in her life when a woman I had not seen before walked in looking a little bit frazzled. She was about 10 minutes late to the meeting, and this was just not acceptable in our world. Everything stopped. Jane looked at this woman and if looks could kill this woman would be long gone by now.

My boss, my mentor, my idol, looked at this poor frazzled woman and stated 'You're late.' The woman nervously responded 'Jane, I'm sorry, I just put my new baby in childcare. It is my first day back today after six weeks' maternity leave, and it was the first time I had to leave her with anyone. I just wanted to make sure she settled ok.' She was crying the whole time she was speaking, which didn't seem to bother Jane because she just responded 'If you want this job, take your kid to childcare, drop them off, and be at my meeting on time. This job is what is going to give your child their future, don't forget that. If you don't respect this job, then you don't deserve to be here.' The poor woman just sat down and silently wept throughout the whole meeting. I have always wondered what she was thinking in that meeting because I am sure it wasn't anything to do with what we were discussing.

At that very moment, I made the decision that I was not going to be like my mentor and idol at all. The image of Jane is what I thought I wanted and needed out of life, but it was that moment that made me realize that I wanted to be a mother more than anything. I wasn't willing to sacrifice my happiness and my child's happiness for a corporate job that I thought I wanted. A job that I had been working so hard for my whole life.

My own Mom was with me every single day. And although she didn't have a lot of structure to her life, she was there for me. I knew that I could depend on her to always be there. She was my best friend. We laid in the sun together, we put iodine and baby oil on our skin and tanned together. We drank Slim Fast shakes and told each other secrets and we were happy to relax together. My Mom was only 20 years older than me, so when I was fifteen she was only thirty-five. She taught me so much about life. She had the strongest willpower of any woman I had ever known and she had heart, she wasn't afraid to love or be loved. In this respect, I wanted to be like my Mom. For the longest time I had rebelled against everything that she stood for, I thought she was the last person to idolize because she didn't have money or power. But in a split second, in that meeting, all of my priorities changed and I realized that maybe my Mom had sacrificed money and power and jobs so she could be at home with me. I still wanted money and power, but I was no longer willing to pursue it at the cost of everything else.

Mom didn't have as much drive as me, many people don't, but I wanted it all. I decided that I would have the best of both worlds. I would be Jane and my Mom combined. I could be a strong, successful, rich business woman, that still spent her time nurturing and looking after her child and family. The first thing I had to do was organize my priorities. What did my perfect life look like? I wanted to be in a high role position, run a company for myself, have my baby with me, travel, inspire other people, make enough money to live comfortable and want for nothing, have time for my husband and make sure we stay great friends and not just partners in a life that we created but don't participate in.

At that moment, I made the decision that I was never going to put my child in daycare. That I was going to raise a family and not rely on other people to do it for me. I would still have a multiple six-figure life, and six-figure business but my family would be there with me every step of the way.

At this time in our life, Brian and I were sleepwalking through life. We both had great jobs, we had a new house, but we weren't connecting with or enjoying it. Sleepwalking through our days. We would both wake up early in the morning having our own focus. One of us would go surfing, and the other would head off to the gym. We were never together. We'd each come back in hustle mode, ready to start our personal days. We both had a long commute and would be sat in traffic traveling to and from work. We weren't living for us; we were only living up to the standard of what we both thought society expected of us to be deemed successful.

Once I made these realizations life wasn't as fun and fun-loving anymore. It was getting harder and harder every day to face the life that I have created for myself. So one day I came home and said to Brian 'Let's organize a dinner together.' He was completely shocked by this request and was like 'What?' That night over dinner I told him that 'I never want to put our child in daycare and I want to have a child so I am quitting my job.' He was dumbfounded. 'You've got to be freaking kidding me' he said. 'We just bought a $1.4 million home with 5 bedrooms so you could start a family and now you want to quit your job. I don't care if I become my bosses, bosses, boss I'm never going to make enough money to fulfill the life that we have planned out.' I calmly said to him 'I am going to figure this out.'

I had just watched a documentary on Steve Jobs and he had said that the world is moving to the Internet. People were actually building businesses online. "The world is moving to the internet. People are going to be building businesses online. They're going to be building their life online, and they're going to move to the internet. If you are not part of this new wave, then you're going to miss out." This really resonated with me and I decided that that was how I was going to have the best of both worlds. I could be a Jane and be a Mom all at the same time without having to sacrifice anything.

10

The Beginning Of A New Life

This was all back in 2005 when the Internet was just starting to blow up. Facebook, YouTube, none of these social media sites were around at this point. WordPress and blogging had only just started to become popular. I didn't even really understand what it was all about at the time, but the documentary with Steve Jobs really stuck with me, and I thought if this guy was making such a big deal about it maybe it was worth giving it a go. I started to researching business models, franchises, brick and mortar and things online, I would type in words like 'work at home mom.' All kinds of different websites popped up to my surprise.

As with anything that you put your focus to, good or bad, you start to see examples and signs of it everywhere. I would be listening to the radio and hear an interview with people working from home; there were commercials on TV about it, and there was an abundance of information online about it. I really started to believe that this thing was for real. One call back list in particular caught my eye and I decided to leave my name and phone number on it to get more information.

So I put my email address in, and a woman called me to tell me about the business. She asked me why I wanted it, but she was a really poor prospector, I just wanted her to get to the point. There I was, my ego was so big that I didn't even want to listen to her, I just wanted to bypass her and get to the information. When in reality I needed that woman so badly, I needed the movement that she made, I needed her energy, and that is exactly what people do in business, they want to skip over the important stuff, which is what I did.

Anyway she put me on a call, and I found out it was a personal development program, in direct sales. I didn't know what MLM meant - my first prospecting calls I had people asking me if this was MLM and I had no idea what that was, nor did I understood why they would ask but realized it was a business model that people were searching for at the time. So I spent $1500 on a personal development program, and I thought I could make $1000 on this thing and it could change my thinking, I was in.

Seven days later they had a four-day event in Anaheim. This was December, and it was snow season, I said to Brian 'hey we've got to go to this business thing', and he said 'You're crazy, I'm going snowboarding,' I hadn't told him much about it. So he went snowboarding, and I went to the meeting. There were 3000 people in a room, and I couldn't believe it.

I was completely enamored that there were that many people interested in the exact same thing I was; FREEDOM. After listening to the speakers and successes I just said, 'Put me on the list; I'm in' a $24,700 investment. Now remember we'd just bought our first million dollar home and it sounded like we were making a lot of money. We were, but we had our money invested in properties and we living the 'treadmill' lifestyle, so we didn't have a lot of cash. So I called ... credit card cos ... extended myself and I had just enough to invest ... and didn't tell Brian.

Yes, you read that right, I didn't tell Brian. When he returned from boarding he asked me what we did, and I told him 'They're going to teach me some marketing, and how to connect with people, I'm gonna call these people,

I'm gonna get leads, I'm gonna call them and just use the system.' Simple right? He said 'That sounds friggin retarded, what's wrong with you, you have an MBA!' So that's where it all started.

I started studying Google AdWords and bought a copy of Perry Marshall's AdWords book where I learned that people are looking purchase a hole, not a drill, and all about attraction marketing and how to solve people's problems over selling them something. So I started doing Google AdWords and newspaper ads and got really good at them, I would sit with my credit card on my desk and place google ads and what do you know, people would respond!

> 'Work at home Mom,
>
> don't believe me,
>
> don't call!'

And I would get a bunch of leads and call them in my lunch time, come home, lock myself in my office and I would just call, call, call. I was on a mission. For three months I called 3000 leads, and I didn't make one sale!! Brian kept opening the door and asking, have you made a sale yet, have you made a sale yet? He still didn't know I'd spent almost $25,000 he just thought it was the $1500. He thought I was crazy; I thought I was crazy, but I just had to figure this thing out.

Three months in there was an event in Cancun.

I knew I had to make a go of this; I was determined. So I went on a mission, and I did one thing in Cancun that made a difference. I asked every successful person there 'What is the one thing that you did that created your success?' And these answers became the foundation of my 8 Phases of Leadership. Also, someone told me, if you keep putting dollar signs on people's foreheads they're going to run from you because then it's all about you and selling them things, so stop selling, if you sell you repel. So we're here to change lives, and we have the opportunity along the way so let's help people think differently, help them to understand what entrepreneurialism is, help them understand what business is and help them realize they could do it 'non-traditionally.'

I got it!

This was my lightbulb moment. So I spoke to lots of great leaders, and I went up to the owner and said 'I'm going to be your top income earner!' and he said, yeah lots of people say that let's see what happens.

So we went home, and I did not want to go to my JOB anymore, I was working, going through the motions, and thought this is a killer. Here's the difference - I'd get on the calls now with a totally different mindset. I'd ask 'OK so you've got kids, how does it feel not being able to be home with your kids? Would you like to be home with your kids? Do you see that as a possibility?' 'No' 'OK well what if there was a way you could be home with your kids and still earn a similar income, but now you're home with your kids and using the Digital Economy?' After being asked that question and having the realization they could have it all, they started saying 'Yes'. This was start of our success.

Checks started arriving in the mail like hotcakes. I was getting $1500 and keeping $997 and sending the company the rest. I kept saying 'Brian this is amazing!' Next minute I was on a call and this person wanted the whole thing and sent me a check for $24,700. And I'd just made $10k and all of those other sales, so I walked out to Brian and said 'You're not going to believe this, I've just made $36,000!' and he was like 'What?' Because he had been horrible, even after the Cancun event, he was over it all. He was saying, you're better than this, you're a corporate executive, you have a better mindset than this, get to your job back. After this, I went to my boss, Jane, and quit my job; she said there's no way this is going to work; you'll be back begging for your old position, and I told her no way.

I left that meeting and went right to the Mercedes-Benz dealership and told them, I wanted to buy my very first real car. I had been driving company minivans for years and I was ready to go ALL IN. So, sure enough, I get my very first CLK convertible, Mercedes and was on top of the world because I knew I could do it and believed in myself.

This was the big breaking point of our lives.

11

We Are Crushing It!

"What Doesn't Kill You

Makes You Stronger"

So now I've quit my JOB and Brian decides to keep his, now we can see evidence that this business I am building, this online world has great potential for us. I'm taking care of everything, I'm marketing, making sales calls, things are building, and they're growing. I've been invited to speak and share my story with people, going to one day events and speaking on stages. I'm really developing myself, growing my mind, journaling every day, and things are really blooming.

Now at this time we decided to sell our first house we ever bought (we had kept it when we bought our $1.4M house and we profited over $500,000 from it. So business was booming, we had big profits from this house, and we decided to invest in a real estate development. It was like one of those divine intervention moments. One of those real defining moments that have you wondering why the universe put this person in front of you, or this incident. It's like sliding doors, one of those moments when you take one door and then all of a sudden a million different doors open, and this was one of those moments.

I had just got off a big call, was celebrating my wins as a top producer in this company, and I was walking through Wholefoods when I bumped into an old friend Bill, a friend I hadn't seen in years. We asked each other how we were and he told me he was now a financial adviser and getting involved in real estate deals in Arizona. And I said 'Wow that's great!' and offered to share the information with me. And at that moment because everything was working so well for us, I was open to every opportunity. An opportunity, I was like 'Opportunity yeah! (fist pumping) Bring it my way.'

So he came over and shared with Brian and me how he'd connected with the top developers in the West Coast, and how they had ten positions open. This was going to turn into about a $50M deal over the next several years, and they were looking for investors to take it on.

Brian and I were like, we're killing it, we just made half a million dollars with the sale of our first house, all because Brian's dad had left him a nest egg and we were able to buy the home we were now in.

Side note here - a lot of people thought we had made it because we had such good corporate jobs, but it wasn't. It was because Brian's dad had died of AIDS and left us a lot of money and my drive came from my drug-addicted father and how not to be like him. We didn't have a big golden spoon; we had to chew on glass to get to that moment.

So the timing was perfect. We had a huge cash lump sum, and we had to invest it somewhere, so we didn't have to pay huge capital gains, and now, I was thinking, we can take ourselves to the very next level.

So Bill introduced the whole idea to us, he shared the entire development. This time, I'll be very honest, we were so very green and so ignorant. It all sounded great; it sounded amazing, we were thinking we can't lose so let's meet this developer.

We've got several hundred thousands of dollars waiting to be invested somewhere, we're in this million dollar home, business is crushing it, Brian still has a job, easy decision making, LET'S DO IT!

So we invested a few hundred thousand, there was a total of 23 homes, and we had our names on 16 of them. And our name was on the construction loan of these homes. We also had 6 or 8 very close people in this development with us, friends and family.

Things were going great, we were developing for over a year and a half, this guy was taking us on yachts, he was taking us out for expensive dinners, we were going to Arizona and staying in these beautiful homes. The idea was to create this Masters Club of real estate; everything was great!

Then I find out I'm pregnant, yeah I'm going to have a baby! I'd invested my life for the Unstoppable Family (which wasn't existing yet), and life could not be any better.

We were so green that we allowed Bill to sign off on our names on all the construction loans to make it easy and so why not just give the rights to the developer to take money out whenever he needed it for the construction loans. So everything was ticking along smoothly until I was about seven months along with Hanalei and things started to get weird. We knew the construction loans were coming up in a couple of months and Brian went out to the development. There was no water in the homes, there were no toilets, they were still under construction. They were nowhere near homes yet, and the construction loans were coming up in 3 months, and you have to be 70% complete under the loans, and there was absolutely no money left. They (the bank) were like well you've taken the money out, and then we realized that he (Bill) was just a con artist, very, very slick.

So at this point, we start to realize that things are going bad, really, really bad. We were just trying to deal with it, but I was getting really stressed and at the same time trying to focus. On the 33rd day before Hanalei was due my waters broke. I was actually on a call introducing one of our business calls, and I was hosting it and said 'You know what, I need to go my water just broke.' I turned to Brian, and I was like 'Oh my gosh my water broke.'

Here I was 33 days before I was due and I am in labor. I called my midwife and I asked 'What do I need to do?' She said 'Let me call you back.' I was like 'why are you calling me back; you're my midwife.' She called be back and told me 'I can't deliver Hanalei legally in California.' I said to her 'What are you talking about? You are my midwife I have been using you the whole time.' She explained that in California a midwife is not capable of delivering a child that early because of potential complications. So I thought holy shit you have to be kidding. I didn't want to have the baby in the hospital because I didn't know anything about the hospital. Everything we had been doing was in preparation to have the baby at home. I really didn't want to have the baby in the hospital, but I had no choice.

We went to Scripps Hospital in La Jolla; it is probably the nicest hospital in the world to have a baby. We went in and proceeded to tell them that she is early and that I didn't want any medication nor did I want anyone to touch me. The doctor came in he didn't really know how to handle it. In California, 75% schedule a C-section and 82% of them have an epidural. So this hospital has no idea how to deliver a baby naturally, and they have no idea how to deal with a woman that doesn't want them to touch them.

More power to what me this Unstoppable Momma. Here I am ready to have this baby, and she is progressing super slow. They come in and check on me. We have an acupuncturist. Brian has The Grateful Dead playing; we are listening to books, watching movies, talking to friends. It has been 12 hours and still no baby. They are saying it has been a long time and she is not progressing. They give me this fear factor that I need this Pitocin. It will increase my labor. It won't hurt the baby; it won't go in her blood brain barrier. It is not a medication; it is just a hormone that is naturally created by your body but given to by injection to progress labor. I was fighting them all the way.

Finally, after pushing and prodding, they decided to give me Pitocin and my midwife persuaded me to do it. Then the contractions started to come. It is getting tight and unbearable. As any woman would know it is friggin insane in labor. My labor was chaos. They kept coming in. They came in and told me their epidural guy was leaving soon so if I wanted to get an epidural I would have to do it there and then because he wouldn't there in an hour. I felt like I was going to die and that was when they gave me it because they know you will do anything then. I look at Brian and my friend and my Doula (midwife). It was getting tough now. I was like I have committed, No no no. Sure enough, they jammed me; they maxed me out on Pitocin. My body starts squeezing and squeezing and squeezing; it is like hell.

To make a long story short, my Mom arrived from Michigan. After I had been in labor for 15 hours and the baby starts to come, and I start to push her out as hard as I can. I popped all of the blood vessels in my eyes. The doctor said he couldn't believe that I did that, that I just went through labor with the amount of Pitocin I was on. Women were coming into the room, shaking my hand saying 'You are the natural birth that had so much Pitocin.' No one could believe that I had had a natural birth because women just don't do it anymore. That was a crazy powerful, unstoppable momma style. My eyes are fully bloodshot, but I have this perfect baby.

Now I am going to share this, this is the coolest conception story. We got home, and after a couple of weeks Brian posted a picture - this is really cool we call this conception rock. No one really knew except for this one guy who is from Sedona, and he said 'Wow Brian do you know what that is?' Brain said "yeah it is in Sedona it is a cool rock.' But he was like 'No, do you know what that rock is called that you are standing on?' He said it is called 'Kachina Woman and it is the most powerful vortex in the world. It is in Sedona. Your daughter was conceived on top of the strongest energetic field in the world' Saying this gives me goosebumps because it makes me realize that my child is so special, powerful and amazing. She chose us; she chose us to be her parents at that moment, at that time. And so this story of us trying to have babies and traveling and then finding out we are losing everything, we have this magic child.

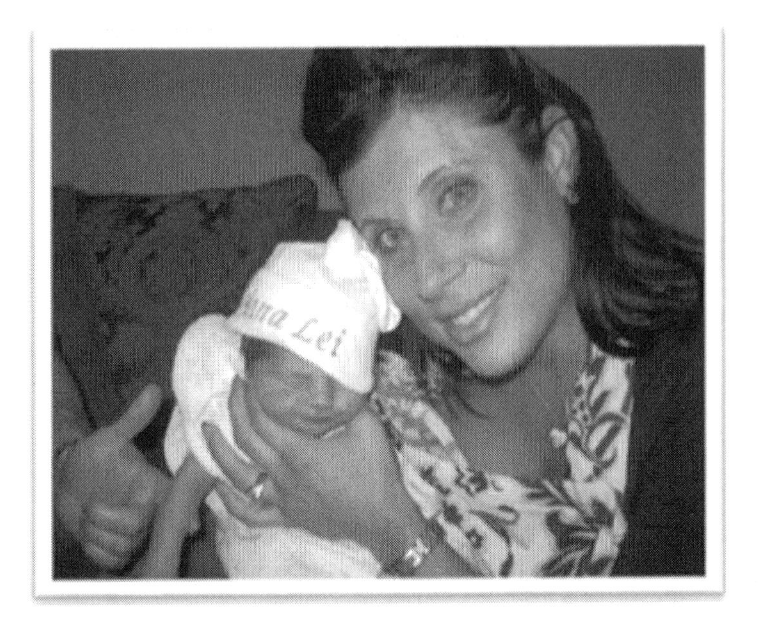

After having and natural birth and returning home with beautiful Hanalei we now realized that everything is going away. Brian was getting a lot of calls, we were talking to a lot of lawyers, attending a lot of meetings, and all we hear is 'You guys are screwed! This guy is a big master plan, he took your money, took your name, and now you're on the hook."

My stress was high, and I had the baby early because we were losing everything. We were spending more on the lawyer and now we were up shit creek. All of our partners were just fighting it and fighting it. After all this stress how do you teach prosperity consciousness, how do you sell people on making money when you have none. You are standing in a $1.4 million home, it costs $12,500 just to breathe in that house. Just to breathe, not to eat or have fun. So our net was

$25,000 a month to live. How do you offer that to anyone when you can't even afford skype credit?

We were in a pickle. We were super stressed, and things started to fade really fast. This is when it gets really cool.

> "You will attract everything that you require. If it's money you need you will attract it. If it's people you need you'll attract it. You've got to pay attention to what you're attracted to, because as you hold images of what you want, you're going to be attracted to things and they're going to be attracted to you. But it literally moves into physical reality with and through you. And it does that by law."
>
> **Bob Proctor**

Being a mother is the highest paid job in the world, since the payment is in pure love!
Like this if you agree!
#UnstoppableMomma

12

The $5 Burrito

"If you change the way you look at things,

the things you look at change!"

Wayne Dyer

So there I was with my brand new baby, at home sitting in her perfect velvet chair, her whole room was white and pink, and I looked up at the ceiling. I had hand painted all these cherub angels all over the ceiling, and they were holding little flags saying Prosperity, Abundance, Love, Joy, and Trust, and I can remember sitting in this chair thinking boy, you've got to be kidding me … everything I've worked for, everything I've believed in, everything I was doing.

And now this baby is here, I've built this business, and finally this baby is here, and I'm in a worse position than I was when I went into that meeting with Jane. All along, we're being taken by this criminal developer who's taken our green name, our naivety, used our cash and our name, and put us on every million-dollar home note. Our names were on about twenty-three homes, and he was stealing from us the whole time, while I have this new baby.

I'm thinking 'now what are we going to do?' Do we go back to a JOB, go back to corporate, back to Jane, because I can make $350,000 a year, does Brian go back to being an engineer, just what are we going to do?

Our lawyers told us, if we don't file for bankruptcy it's just going to be horrible. We went through almost a full year going through this process until the lawyers finally said you're going to spend 100s of 1000s of dollars and you're never going to win, he's just going to drain everyone. So we finally agreed to sign our name off everything, we were exonerated from all debt because we had such good credit and it was a fraud situation.

We signed our names off of over $16m all the homes, our personal home, all our debt; we didn't owe a thing because we were able to prove that we were defrauded. The only thing we had to pay back was our student loans and the money we took out of our IRA; the government didn't see that as a loss. So we still owed the US Government over $100,000 in penalties. We were paying taxes and student loans. They cleared our name, and we were able to keep our new $1.7M house. So we said yes, let's just stay in our house, with our baby, we have our business, a Mercedes in the driveway; we have a new Escalade now; we can stay here and keep building this life ...

So we were fighting for this, fighting for that, our payments on our house were $12,500 a month alone, it wasn't cheap. We were living that 'perfect high life,' and I'm fighting Brian, fighting myself, wanting all these things, and at that moment sitting in that chair looking up at the cherubs I think to myself, 'what are you doing? Who do you think you are, what representation are you going to be for this little girl? You fought for this, are you going to stay, are you going to go back to what you said you'd never do, break the vow you made for her or are you going to fight for it?'

'You know what you're doing

You have a structure

You've done it before

You can do it again!'

I thought, yes I can do this.

It had been three months when one day we were all lying in bed together. Brian was so sick to his stomach because he had his parents take part of their retirement funds and invest into this development, he had friends invest into this develop-ment, and they lost everything, and his family were totally stressed out. Brian doesn't even know how to talk to them about it. Most of his friends didn't want to talk to us because it's like we should have told them. We were just sitting by ourselves saying what are we going to do?

So Brian and I are talking, and I say look we can do this, we've done it before, we can do it again. And Brian says, Yes ... I don't know. I want you to read this chapter (he was reading Tim Ferris's The Four Hour Work Week) about taking a mini-retirement, I think we should just sell everything and leave. I was like 'FUCK you! No way, don't you dare, we've got a baby, I'm fighting for this, I just made a decision, I'm going to do this, I'm going to rebuild this! I've got a home, I've got a car, I've got this, I've got that, I'm going to stand up for what I believe in ...' and he was 'No we're going to sell it all, we're just going to sell it and leave.'

I was so pissed with him I didn't talk to him for 24 hours, and we were in bed, and he asked me again just to read this chapter about taking a Mini-Retirement. How about we're not leaving, we're just going to take a mini-retirement and go away for say two years. You can still work your business; we can still figure some things out. Brian says to me Bali Indonesia would be an amazing place because we had been there on a surf trip with our surfing buddies, back in the day and he says remember Bali, we never really explored it, wouldn't it be really cool if we went back and really explored it. Anyway, he went to bed, and by the morning I had read the whole book, all about how to systematize your business and go travel. Well, I thought, we kind of already have our business all systematized, all I do is put people on these calls, and it's all virtual, and I thought I could do this. I started getting deeper involved, deeper and deeper and I thought OMG we could do this. By the time Brian woke up, I was researching Bali, and he looked at me and said 'You get it, don't you!'

So I started putting systems in place, so our business could be run. We hired his parents as our 'grounds home office'. So all bills are sent to them, they scan them in and tell us if they're important, they send them to us via email. They have a credit card, bank account access and checks, anything they need they have access to. His sister became our bookkeeper.

So we think OK this is going to work. We talked to our agent, and we decide to short sell our house, this is in May (month 4). In June we decide we're going to travel the world for two years. June 3rd on my birthday and popped bottle of Opus 1 from of my best friends Laurie Ioquinta and we'd saved it for a special day. So we popped this to announce to everyone we were going traveling.

Next, I started googling all of the places where I would want to live, where we could visit and I thought of the program Brian wrote called 'How To Create Your Perfect Day'. This is what Brian had written down,

> *'Surfing every day, traveling around the world for the world's best waves, having a child with you, enjoying life, smiling and running a business virtually.'*

That was his perfect day, and I thought yeah that sounds cool because that is what we'd been creating. So I was going through this chapter and my perfect day started to pop up in my head and oh my god ... I could be with this child, so much time as I have wifi, there's Skype now, I could call people literally anywhere, it's for real!

This was June 5th 2 days after my 35th birthday, we opened a bottle of Opus 1 Cabernet, which my girlfriend had given me the year before, but I hadn't opened it because I didn't feel we had enough reason to, and declared 'we're taking our mini-retirement 2 year trip around the world. We're selling this big huge monstrosity of a home, sell all our cars'. Because after reading the 4 Hour Work Week, I thought what are we doing, all we've become is materialistic. And now our representation for our new baby is - collect a lot of things and stay in this huge house, I'm going to raise a southern California American styled child that doesn't value things. And I realized that I was becoming shallow and was not being the mother that I said I was going to be ... stay here and build up your business was just selfish of me, it was my ego and my fear that I couldn't do it again and that was the big switch.

So we made this big decision, and at the same time, we were losing everything. The banks were still coming after us. We had every different crazy ringtone possible for every single debt or debtor that was calling, and we were just trying to ignore the ringer. So then how were we supposed to help others make money while our mindsets were in the toilet, we were trying to move forward and talking about prosperity mindset, and we were not prosperity conscious right then.

So we were going through our own turmoil and our own personal development and realizing that we are NOT our bank account and our bank account does not make us who we are. We make us who we are. Who we are is our character and just because our bank account doesn't represent it, doesn't mean that's not who we are. So I had to get really clear on those things and when I did we were still losing things. We had to pay huge monies to the lawyers for the bankruptcy alone; we now didn't even have any Skype credit; our families didn't have money to lend us, and without Skype credit, we couldn't run our business. So now we had to find a way to make money because the business wasn't selling because our minds were in the toilet, how are we going to get out of this?

Every morning we'd get on our bikes and ride down the hill to the beach to a coffee shop, so we were in a better environment, and just get on our phones. One day I was riding down with Hanalei to the coffee shop, Brian was already there and I got an email that said 'You have insufficient funds in your bank account.' I told Brian, and he said he'd just got a $5 burrito. I'm like what? You got a $5 burrito that took our bank account into the red. At this point, I was flipping out. Here we were in the middle of San Diego, losing everything, still in our $1.7M home and we were fighting over a $5 burrito.

Here's the reality you need to understand, there was so much going on around us, there are so many facades that you never really know what's going on in someone's life, you never know what they're going through. This is why getting connected to humans and bringing back our humanity, our connection to people will help us all grow; it's vitally important. We get stuck on our phones, stuck on the internet, and we forget to create the human connection again.

So we're standing on the boardwalk, and I was flipping out, and we're fighting over a $5 burrito because my husband needed to eat some food, which meant we went over on our bank accounts and we've turned into fighting devils. I take off, and Brian was still standing there. There was a man standing in front of a beautiful oceanfront multi-million dollar home, and he says to Brian "Hey man, come here' 'I saw your wife and your baby, congratulations you have a baby' and Brian just said 'Yeah thanks, Dude' then Brian said, 'can I ask you something?' and he said 'yeah sure'. Brian asked 'have you ever had things go so bad in your life that you're not sure where to turn, that you just don't know what's going on?' and he replies 'Absolutely, about 7 or 8 times I've gone bankrupt and now I'm standing here in this beautiful home that you see me in, and I'm losing this house. And I'm trying to figure out a way I can keep this house and my properties. And my wife doesn't like to come here anymore because it's a representation of our losses.'

He goes 'Wow, my wife and I have just had a huge fight because we just found out we've lost everything, our home, and just had a baby and I just had a $5 burrito, and we're fighting over it.' He said 'Yeah I'm in the same boat,' Brian said 'I never of thought that, you look so happy, you look so great.' And he said 'yeah I'd never have thought that about you guys either. I see you every day riding your bikes with your new baby and thinking, wow that family's got it good. I'm here, and my wife won't talk to me, and you say your wife's pissed at you. You need to talk to your wife because you guys can do this.'

So we're in the same scenario, we think everything's great with him, and he thinks everything is great with us. Brian came back and said let's make a plan. So we planned to sell everything, a fire sale, let's just sell it, let our egos go. Our friends were all corporate executives, and they all judged us, we never judged them, but they were like 'told you so.' Either our egos got in the way, or they thought they had and that we were a little bit cocky, and that's all they saw, and now we can never really connect with them again, they were saying 'yeah, thought that was going to happen.' Their lives were moving on.

We made our plan and put up an estate sale sign, people were just ransacking our home, and we sold everything, from the Bugaboo stroller to the pink little swivel chair for Hanalei, china from our wedding, paintings and we sold absolutely everything for just about dirt, we just about gave it all away. And we had $23,548 left to our name. We left with a dream and a vow.

It was six months from when we made that declaration, and we had six months to get out of dodge. We put the house up for a fast sale and started planning how we were going to get away. We decided that we weren't going to escape from life, but create a life that we didn't have to escape from. And on 25 November we left San Diego, sold everything we had. We had five bags to our name, two surfboards and Brian had to take his Escalade to the repo.

He asked if he could deliver it the next morning as we had to get to the airport. Brian dropped us off at the airport and delivered the Escalade, and the guy gave him a lift back to the airport. He was 'Wow man, what did you guys do, did you win the lottery so that you can go traveling around the world?' Brian said 'No we filed for bankruptcy - you're taking my car!' He said 'Can I get your card?' So funny those prospective moments that change for people, and it changed for us.

There we were standing at the airport, on our way to Hawaii. We left on 25th so we could be in Hanalei Bay for 28th to celebrate our 5th anniversary. The funny thing is it took five years for the 28th to fall on the day after Thanksgiving, the same as when we got married. So it was pretty magical time and it meant the universe was telling us this was the right time and allows us to remember that when things happen you have to be open, you have to know that things will happen to you in your life and if you are open it and be aware it can be the best things that happens to you.

So we get to Hanalei Bay, Brian was determined to put Hanalei in Hanalei Bay at one year old and put her feet in the water on a wave. And that's what we did, we got her a boogie board and put her on a wave.

And that's what we did.

That's how this journey started.

The first day of our journey

And that was the beginning of our two-year trip, that we are still continuing, and we will be starting our ninth year this November.

13

Brian's Perspective

Mini Retirement

I want to give you a little bit of insight into how I was thinking and where my mind was when we were at our lowest point. Rhonda will talk about it in depth of course but this just my perspective.

When we knew that we were losing everything, when we invested big time, before the Four Hour Work Week. Tim Ferris's book kept coming up with the mini-retirement. I kept thinking we are going to have file bankruptcy, we are going to have to start over. I said to Rhonda what if we just got rid of everything and travelled around the world? She thought I was frigging crazy.

But a month and a half after that conversation the audio book that I was listening to about packing up and traveling around the world came back to the exact same spot. Even though I had read the book three or four times over it was this one time where the audio came to me and I was really listening.

I never really paid attention to what Tim Ferriss was saying before this moment but just then I thought to myself that the smartest thing we could do would be to pack up, sell everything and just travel the world. Again Rhonda was in her stressed mood and just looked at me like I was crazy. I was getting used to this in my life by this point.

Another month goes by and my phone started to play the audio book in that exact same spot again. I knew that I had to get her to listen this time. Hanalei was one-year-old and fast asleep. I told her to listen to this audio, don't argue with me, don't ask me anything about it, just listen. I told her that I was going to bed and that we could chat about it in the morning.

I woke up at 2am and found that my wife wasn't in bed with me. I went downstairs to get a drink of water and to check on her. I walked into the kitchen and there was Rhonda sitting at the computer researching Bali. I thought to myself 'Yes, we are going to make it!

"The truth is that there is no actual stress or anxiety in the world; it's your thoughts that create these false beliefs. You can't package stress, touch it, or see it. There are only people engaged in stressful thinking."

Wayne Dyer

Life in Bali, Brian, Hanalei, Jubril, scooters and rice fields, oh and freedom!

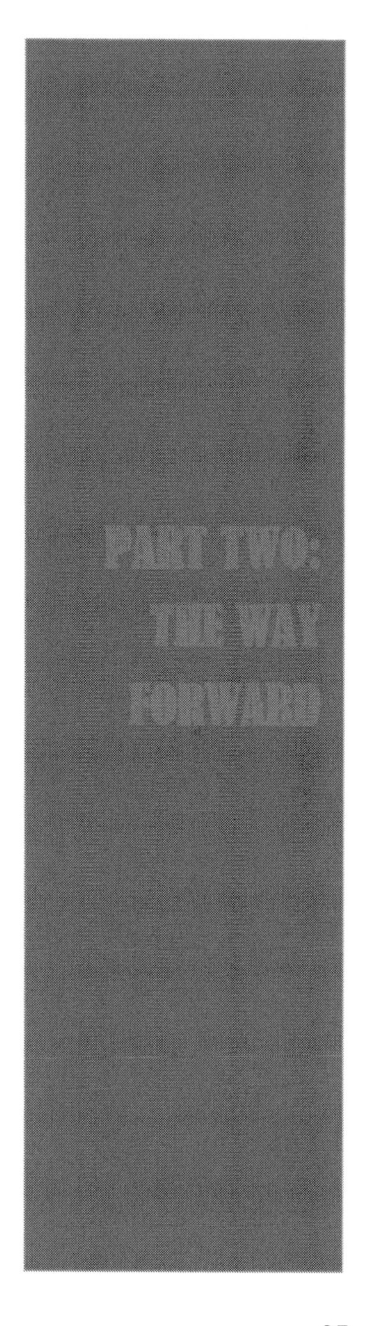

PART TWO: THE WAY FORWARD

BEHIND
EVERY
SUCCESSFUL
WOMAN IS
HERSELF

14

Change Your Thoughts, Change Your Life

As introduction to this second part of my book, I'd love you to listen to a recording between myself, Wayne Dyer and Deepak Chopra.

It is always vitally important to have mentors and people to follow in life and in business, but even more so when the going gets tough. This was a very special moment when I called into Deepak Chopra radio show with special guest, Dr Wayne Dyer for spiritual guidance as we were going through a financial and emotional crisis at the time we realized we were losing everything.

In the brief 5 minute conversation, Wayne Dyer gave us 3 lessons that will stick with us forever. Here are his direct messages to Rhonda...

- "No one can make you upset, depressed, hurt, anxious, or fearful without your consent."
- "The worst things in life turn out to be the most important steps that you need to take, in order to get to the next place in your life."
- "The highest place you can get to with this individual is to practice forgiveness, instead of revenge & anger"

Deepak Chopra and Wayne Dyer radio show 28 July 2007

Go to https://www.youtube.com/watch?v=eHVyk85cLwg

to listen to the recording on YouTube.

15

Why Live An Unstoppable Life?

"If you don't design your own life plan,

chances are you'll fall into someone else's plan.

And guess what they have planned for you? Not much."

Jim Rohn

My intention when writing this book was to help give you vision and purpose that everything is possible. No matter what cards we are dealt in life, we can always create and live an unstoppable life. Being unstoppable means going for everything you want out of life and not letting anything get in your way, including yourself. It means seeing situations and being confronted with times that are really tough but knowing that you can get through them. The easiest way is to do this is to back up, go back to the point where you felt comfortable, and to go back to what you know. Go to your authentic truth and then you will be unstoppable.

I have a saying, and I want you to remember it and live by it - 'Get out of your own stinking thinking!' We are our own biggest saboteurs and if you listen to those voices in your head that tell you that your past determines your future you are not living an unstoppable life. You don't have to conform to society's expectations; there are no laws that say you have to work a 9 til 5 job straight out of college, or that you should get married and have children right away. You don't have to live up to your parents' expectations of you. You are an individual, and you deserve so much more out of life. You just have to start believing in yourself. Be authentic to who you are and what you want, that is how you live an unstoppable life.

Belief starts from you looking yourself in the mirror and asking yourself, "Can I do this? Do I believe in myself? Have I done it before? Have other people been able to do this?" When you stop and take the time actually to see what is happening around you, it will become apparent that anything is possible. Talent alone is not the answer; it is the drive and passion within you that will allow you to become unstoppable.

You can't give people passion, or drive, or energy, but you can teach them techniques and strategies to empower their lives. Living Unstoppable doesn't need to have a lot of skill. You can actually take an approach that other people are using that I'm going to lay out for you in this book and apply it to your life. Living and being successful starts with you and your own mind, believe it, and it will come!

Now, the inner work begins with you. The Unstoppableness starts within you. The whole statement, "Fake it until you make it," doesn't sit well with me. However, one biological and chemical fact that you need to understand is that your brain doesn't know the difference between things happening and things not happening. When it comes to business, it is not really a good strategy to use, but when you are trying to refocus your brain and mindset it can do wonders for your confidence.

If you see yourself standing in front of a mirror, and you are literally feeling yourself holding up a weight and using a muscle like you're holding up a dumbbell, did you know that your body and your mind knows no difference? Knows no difference whether you're holding that dumbbell or not? Your brain fires. Your neurotransmitters begin to fire, and that tells your brain that you're doing something. That energy is being expended in this area, and your body needs to accommodate for it.

What happens? In the end, you created a result. That means that you can actually fake it until you make it, telling yourself that you can do this, you are successful. You can make it, and your brain will start to believe it. The more and more you start to tell yourself that you can do something, the more your brain will start to follow through on it. The more your body will start to follow through, and your belief will grow.

When you look at yourself and say, "Do I believe in myself?" Say, "Yes. I believe in myself. I can do this." Every single day, I wake up with a mantra, and I talk to myself. I either look in the mirror, or I sit and say, "Rhonda, you are an incredible leader. You inspire people to do great things in their life. You show them that everything is possible. You help more families be free. You must show more families how to get to building a life that they love." This is the essence of belief. When you have a mantra that you tell yourself, you are teaching your brain to believe in the life you want to create for yourself.

I have been saying this same thing with a variation for the last eleven years. I learned it from my dear friend Jim Rohn.

> “Effective communication is 20% what you know and 80% how you feel about what you know.” - Jim Rohn

When you wear the word unstoppable, you hold an armor that tells you that you can. It reminds you every day to be unstoppable. Being unstoppable needs a strong ‘WHY.’ Once you have worked out your WHY everything is possible. I made a vow never to put my child in daycare, all I have to do is look into her eyes and my commitment to the WHY is stronger than ever. What is your WHY?

When I started my job and said I'll never put my child in daycare, that I was going to live out this day, perfect day, every single day, that I was going to quit my job and replace my income, I wasn't going back. There was no plan B. That was my vow and my commitment, and she, Hanalei, became my WHY. Everything I did fueled me to get me to that next step. Everything I did I did because she was my WHY and it was robust enough to keep me motivated and disciplined.

"Discipline is the bridge between goals and accomplishment." - Jim Rohn

As mentioned earlier in this book, at one point in our life we lost everything. I mean everything. We had twenty-three thousand eight hundred and eight dollars and seventy-two cents to our name, and things were looking bad. I could have easily thrown in the towel and made a very convincing argument as to why I needed to go back to the corporate world. I could have reasoned that it would only be for a short time. But I had the armor; I already had the mindset of being unstoppable and that allowed me to have discipline.

I have a master's degree in business; it would have been so easy for me to get a job that society accepts. But would I have been truthful to myself if I had done that? Did I want the 6 figure income more than I wanted to live an authentic life? NO.

Instead of taking the easy route, I took the harder path. Sometimes the vision and the way forward doesn't always seem so clear, but if you know and believe in yourself that there's gold at the end of that rainbow or there's something at the very end of that path, you're going to do whatever it takes to get through it because your WHY is so strong. You have been telling yourself you can do it; you have been preparing yourself to push through the hard times and to make it to the end of the path.

When you rely on yourself, and have complete faith in your abilities you can create anything you want out of life. You are the only person you can count on to get what you want out of life. You have to believe in yourself, even when everyone around you doubts it. You have to believe that you can do it because no one else is going to do it for you.

I'm unstoppable, and I say that to myself because, it's not always easy, but it's always worth it. When I tell myself I'm unstoppable I believe it. Choose your power word. What does it make you feel like? What is this? Maybe it's peaceful. You need a word that resonates within your soul, something to derive power from. Once you have that word, wear it with pride, wear it like armor, and you too can get through the tough times.

Find a power word that connects with you, so that when you are feeling down, and it's not as easy, you're able to pull yourself through and make things happen. This is the power of being unstoppable. This is the power of taking your life and living it like you want to. There's no hokey pokey. This is real. Tell yourself 'I can', and you will believe it, and once you believe it - it will happen.

This is why I want to write this book. I want to give you strategies. I want to give you hope. I want to give you inspiration and vision through my experiences and my stories. Through my wisdom that I've created.

I also want to give tactical steps to how I've done it, how I just went for it and started building a brand, and started sharing my story, and started having a genuine commitment and belief. How to get it out to the world with tactical techniques and strategies that I have used to not only create a sexy brand but make it so everyone around the world can see it. That's the essence. This is why I am writing this book.

Unstoppable Action Steps

What is your why, what will keep you going when the going gets tough?

____

____

____

Brainstorm words that mean a lot to you and your passion, your mission - what is your power word?

____

____

____

Go to Facebook group and share – www.facebook.com/groups/1FreedomPreneur/

We have sooooo many FREE resources to help you with this at

https://unstoppablemomma.com/bonus for your FREE book resources to help you.

***Nate Buchan** one of our beautiful*

'family members'.

"Think of your life like a movie. You are the main character of your own movie, and you are an actor in other people's movies. It's your responsibility to create the best damn movie you can for yourself and be the best scene in other people's movies."

I came across Brian and Rhonda when I was 19 years old. I saw a video pop up on YouTube of a family that had been traveling round the world for many years. They were living in beautiful locations and working an online business to fund their lifestyle.

It was my DREAM to live like that.

I had just begun a plumbing apprenticeship and was looking to spend the next 40 years crawling under houses and unblocking drains. It freaked me out. So I reached out to them asking for help, and decided to follow in their footsteps. These two people in the photo have literally changed my life on so many levels I find it hard to express in words. I have seen them change the lives of so many people, just like they have for me, I had to ask Rhonda this question.

"How do you consistently stay on top of your game, you always have a vision, loads of energy, you're so giving, and positive. Why is that and how do you do it so consistently?"

She gave me the best piece of advice I have ever heard.

"Think of your life like a movie. You are the main character of your own movie, and you are an actor in other people's movies. It's your responsibility to create the best damn movie you can for yourself and be the best scene in other people's movies. Every time you come into contact with someone, think about how they will feel after meeting you. What kind of scene did you create in their movie, and how are you shaping your movie?

Everything you do, do it for a reason. Be enthusiastic, live with purpose & passion, care for others and be the best you can be. You will look back on your movie knowing you have lived the best and fullest life you possibly can."

When I heard this I suddenly realized that these two people have made some of the best scenes in my movie. From the day I met them they have made an impact on my life and every day I am with them, their energy toward life never waivers.

If you live with this concept and strive to create the best movie for yourself and anyone you come in contact with you will most definitely make a difference in your life and the lives of others. I literally can't thank you guys enough for believing in me more than I believed in myself.

Well it's safe to say Brian and Rhonda Swan have changed my life completely! I flew to Miami to attend one of their live events to meet them in person. They helped me build an online business based around my passions of surf and travel.

I quit my job as a plumber and have been on the road for almost 3 years now. I run my business entirely from my laptop and earn more money than plumbing could ever make me.

I still have to pinch myself. I can't thank you guys enough for your influence and guidance.

Much Love!

Nathan Buchan

Love you guys. This movie is getting better every single day because of you!!

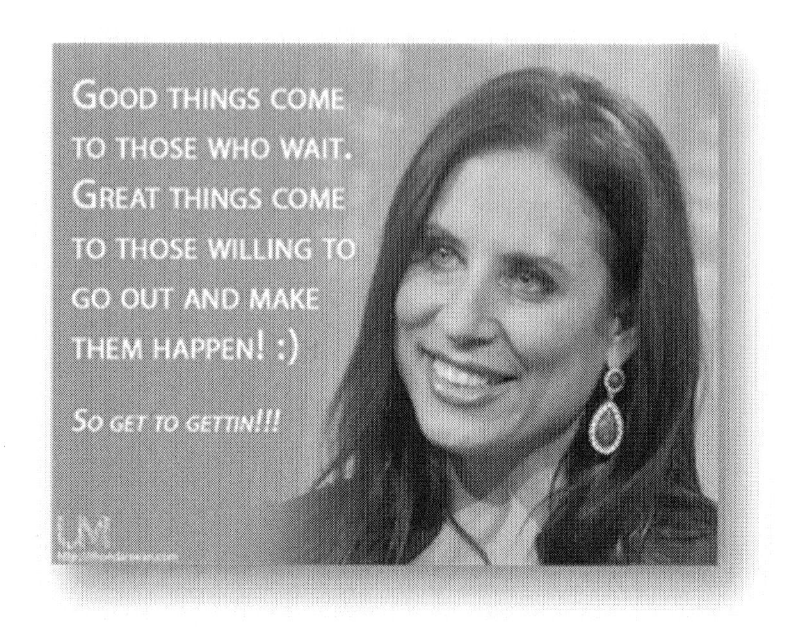
GOOD THINGS COME
TO THOSE WHO WAIT.
GREAT THINGS COME
TO THOSE WILLING TO
GO OUT AND MAKE
THEM HAPPEN! :)
SO GET TO GETTIN!!!

16

Brainstorm, Productize, Monetize, Automate

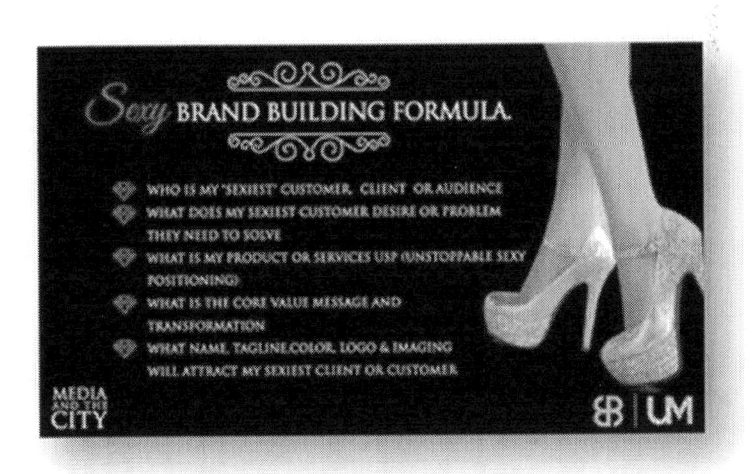

To build a sexy brand you have to have an understanding of the components that that entails. Developing a brand is not just about choosing the right colors or logo or the outside dressing of your business; that is secondary to the overall sexiness of your brand. Of course, it plays a major role in what people see immediately when looking at your brand, but it does not encompass everything you have to think about.

Most people make a decision about your brand within the first three seconds. This initial encounter can be on a website, a video or a product offer you are creating. In those first seconds, you have to make an impression that grabs their attention and ensures they will remember you.

That means having a quality headline and name that people can remember, something that's easy for them to remember, to visualize, and to type. Because if they hear your name and they can't quite understand it, then they're not going to be able to find it. And this is one of the biggest mistakes you can make.

Having a tagline that connects with your audience, something that gives them a mini message about your brand and allows them to connect with it immediately is a fabulous idea. It lets them know what your brand is and what kind transformation they are going to have by choosing you or buying your product.

Make sure that a tagline is no more than 7 to 10 words, because that makes it then a mini message. We want to keep it nice and tight, so people know exactly what they can get from you. Imaging and colors play a significant role in people making decisions.

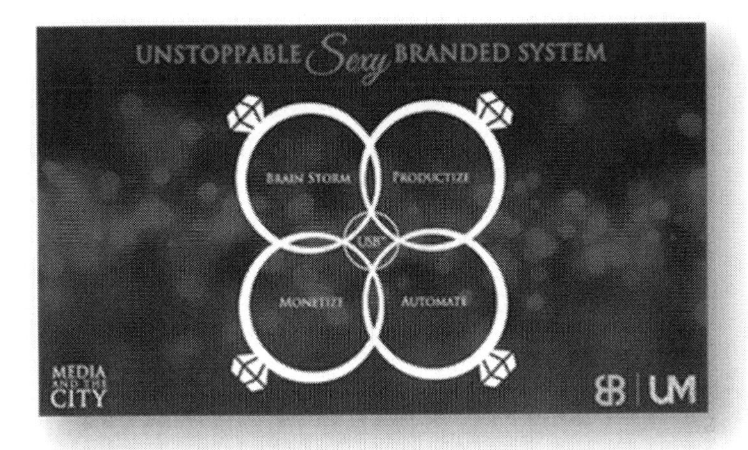

There are four quadrants when encompassing a sexy brand. On the top left side, we have Brainstorm; top right is Productize. Then bottom left is Monetize, and the bottom right is Automate. They're linked together. Directly in the center is your USB, your Unique Sexy Brand. The four quadrants encompass what I like to call your unstoppable sexy branded system. This is what allows you to take your brand out to the world and in front of more people, and get your audience to see you in different components throughout, not only social media but, all media platforms so that you can get your message out to the world in a bigger way.

1 Brainstorm

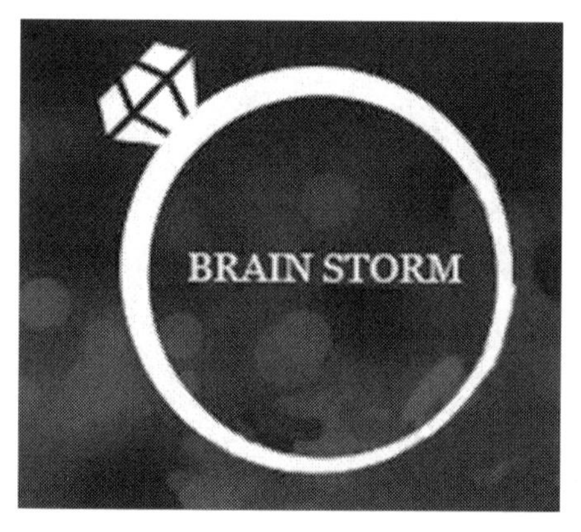

Brainstorming is the new point of any business. It is where you enter the marketplace, where you are discovering what your passion is, what the people want and how to connect with them. When it comes to brainstorming.
I like to do what is called a brain dump. Put 50 ideas on the table of what your passions are that you can turn into profit. This is the discovery and development phase of what you want to offer the world.

It could be a book. It could be a digital product. It could be a coaching program, or it could be a physical product that you feel that the marketplace wants or needs. Just do a major brainstorm. Look at what the market wants. Take a look at your competitors, what are people offering or buying for that matter. Anything and everything that you are passionate about goes on the table, nothing is off limits.

Instead of you being a me-too product, you want to make sure that you stand out. You've got to make yourself unique, which is why we call it your unique business proposition or your unique selling point. That's your USP, which is what makes you stand out over and above the crowd. For instance, McDonald's and Burger King are very similar, but

McDonald's and Burger King have two different core messages and two completely different taglines, right? McDonald's is 'I'm lovin' it.' Burger King's is 'Have it Your Way.' They have a different taste, of course, but more to the point their marketing structure is different. It is their branding and core message that attracts different people to their business.

You want to make sure that what you are doing allows you to be unique and not just like everyone else. When you're brainstorming the products and looking at your competitors and your market match, you want to look at what is it that your customer needs. What is a problem they have that you can solve, and how can you make what you do or have stand out over and above the competition so that you are chosen for your uniqueness and not just by price? Unless you want to be another widget, then you're going to be selected by price, but you can become a higher priced, higher valued product, even though it may be similar to someone else, you add on that additional bonus that keeps people coming back for more. You can use my full program, which I am giving you, as to how to productize and how to sell your product and add more value to it than if you were just to be a me-too product.

Brainstorming time is where you're just brain dumping. Oncc you begin to compare and track what the marketplace wants, now you're able to start making some decisions. What is that product that I can bring to the market that can add value to my niche? To my customer base? Understanding what your niche is will help you when you're brainstorming what that product is. Understanding my very particular niche is that I can target? You have to consider; most people look at generalities when they are creating or selling their products. They're looking at too broad a spectrum, a niche or a group. When you tighten up and understand, 'who your exact customer is, that would buy either this product, this service or this program,' and you know exactly what they're like you will be on the right path to success. I always ask myself these questions. Who is my customer? Are they male? Are they female? What is their age groups? What things do they like to do? Where do they shop? What kind of books do they read? What is the language that they use? Are they travellers? Are they more homebodies? What is their personality?

2 Productize

As you know, there can be a product that somebody wants, but the way it's marketed and talked about can turn off one customer. Let's say, if you are creating a shoe that's called 'badass shoes.' Maybe it is the best product with the best soles, and they're made the best way. But now you have, someone of a religious background that are looking at these shoes, and chances are, the branding is going to be a bit more aggressive than a conservative Christian person would want. You will miss that person altogether. Chances are if you called it 'bad ass,' you're not looking for a Christian, but let's hope that you're not marketing towards them either. What you want to do is niche it in. Who is my exact customer? What are the things that they like? Then when you know who they are, you begin to structure your full brand around it. That's including color. That's including the name. That's including tagline. That's including what connects all the dots.

Start with: What is the product and the program that you think the market will want? Then you define your niche and that particularly targeted niche. Then we reverse engineer it. We decide what we want to talk about, what our skills are, our passions are, what we can provide and what we want to bring out to the marketplace. Then we decide, "Okay, who is our customer now? What does that customer look like? Who is the one customer that we can target?" When you do it this way, it allows you to specifically niche in. You could be targeting 1,000 or maybe 20,000 people. That's a lot of people that are buying your products and your services around the world if you get highly niched into what they want.

Most failures happen in businesses because they become too broad. They target too many people, and then their message is more vanilla than chocolate or strawberry, or raspberry, even better, more focused, right? Now that we know we're looking for our target customer, we're able to begin crafting what our brand message is, what is the core message, and what is it going to look like? Once we start taking our core message, our core customer, we can look at our core story, because our story, of course, is everything. Our story connects us to the people. Your story SHOULD connect with your targeted, focused customer or niche.

For instance, let's say I'm targeting athletes. I was a former athlete. I played softball. I was a high-level athlete, and so let's just say that I am creating a product for athletes. Maybe it's a heartbeat monitor. I decide to create my product and my message, and I want to tell my story. Instead of telling my story about being an athlete that ran and never knew what my heart rate was, or I wasn't getting to my peak performance. I start to tell a story about a woman who travelled the world with her child because she didn't want to put her day care. This is also my story, but it is not one that connects with my customer. Those parts of the story don't match with the particular product or the specific brand. We have to find parts of our story that link, that link people to the product. And not just tell our whole story with no consideration of what our customer is interested in.

Again, we start off with this, what is my brainstorm, what is my market match, what does the market want? Then we go into saying, "What is my specific customer base? What is my core message or the core values that I have that will target my very focused and very specific customer base?" The client base and who I'm targeting is the most important because then we can tailor what our core message is, what are the core values are that our company represents. Begin to build your brand around it, because your messaging and your story will all connect to that one customer. Chances are many products can connect to many people, but you have to start with a core message for a particular client. Then you can expand your circle.

We put our core customer in the middle, and then we make rings around it and overlap into that customer, so the left-hand side might be my core message, the right-hand side circle is my core values. Bottom-left is my story, and the bottom-right is my products. The customer is in the center. All those areas that overlap are the sectors that are directly targeted to your customer. You'll definitely have other marketing campaigns, other areas so that you can target other people, but this specific way allows you to make the customer your focus when you're delivering a product or a service.

Now, some people do it backward, and they end up starting with the product first. They build around the whole product and they try to find the customer. But that's backward, because if you don't know what the market wants, you don't know what's going to be provided to the marketplace and if they want it, then you're going to be developing a product or program that people don't even want. This is a vital piece when it comes to understanding how to start developing a powerful brand. It always starts with the customer.

I'm going to give you some strategies on how to productize that program. Let's look at some strategies on how you can develop and productize a program or a, let's say, a coaching program or a product or service that you may have and you want to be able to release it on the internet. One of my favorite ways to build a product or a program is the 'build the plane while flying it' method. That is one of the best methods that I've used to actually develop my very first product. In fact, I was thrown into the hot coals one time. This is what jump started my whole career in coaching and doing branding workshops.

I was at a three days speakers' event, and it was a speak-to-sell event where everyone that was there was pitching on stage, not only teaching but then they were pitching their products or their services. There were about 35 speakers. I was an attendee of this event so I could learn and see what people had and how they were selling. Sure enough, a woman came on stage, her name was Lisa Sasevic, and she was teaching a way to sell to a lot of people. That was to take your 5 top hottest points that you can teach someone or the transformation that your product or service can offer to someone and package it up and sell it.

She showed her method of how to do that, and it was taking your 5 top things, deep-dive into one, promising that you'll give them more, and then at the end, have them drooling, wanting more, because you only gave them one of the 5. You go deep into that one, and now I call that giving a full entrée of one of your unique selling points, and then having hors d'oeuvres on the other 4, meaning you sample them. You let them take a look at it, taste it a bit, but they don't get it all. In the end, you make the close. You make that full closing offer where it says, 'You can now work further with me by getting my full program.' and then, of course, she invited everyone to come to the back of the room to buy.

I was inspired by that talk. It was such an easy way. I finally realized how easy it could be. Create a unique selling system that has 5 of my core elements that I sell, five areas that I can teach on or help build, go deep into one and then sample the other 4. I'm like, "Wow. This is so simple. I can do this." I figured that I could do this so easily on webinars. I can do this in stages. I can do this at my events to offer long-term coaching. So, sure enough, I spent $1500 on her products, and I went home. Then I got a call from the guy that created the event, and he says, "Hey Rhonda, one of our speakers can't come. Can you speak tomorrow?" Well, sure enough, I said yes, but not only was I nervous, scared, and shitting myself but I was asking myself 'Am I ready for this?'

Productization #1

Build Your Plane While Flying It

One thing about being a professional and stepping into your greatness and being your best you can be is that you've always got to be ready, whether you feel like you're ready or not, you force yourself into the lion's den. You force yourself into getting yourself ready. What I checked with myself is, do I have the right material? I realized I had never really sold from the stage before, but I do have the right material. I can sell, and I can create and develop a program. I took Lisa's product that I had just bought, did a quick 1 hour overview of everything that she taught. Grabbed her manual and created my very first branding workshop that started from developing what is your product or your service, defining who your niche was, creating a core message, and then, of course, dominating on marketing and social media.

I got up on stage. I did exactly what she taught. Told them what I was going to offer upfront. I went deep-dish and deep entrée on one area which was telling your story, and then I sampled all the other 4. Which was understanding who your niche is, how to talk to them, how to define your core message, how to create a brand that connects with people and imaging that connects with individuals, how to choose the right colors? Sure enough, I was the very last person in the room on a Sunday; everyone had been buying thousands of dollars of products, and I sold 70% of the room with my product and developed my very first branding workshop, 4-week workshop. That is how I started building my plane while I was flying it.

Now, this is how I created the product. Was it ready? Not at all. I had just created it. I took five hot points that Lisa said to do, and then I developed a 5-week program. The opening one was like an intro, and then the others were four weeks, and I covered all my main areas, which was building a brand with a tagline and a name, developing your story, finding who your niche was, and then, of course, marketing it with the message to the world. I built my plane while I was flying it. Each week, I would do a recording, and I would put it inside of a small members' area that I created on WordPress.

Now we use ClickFunnels; you can go to –

www.UnstoppableFamily.com/ClickFunnels and get access to the best converting funnel creator and email creator that you can find on the planet. They'll automate your business. I'll go into that in the automation section.

I popped in those recordings. I created a couple of PDFs, and each week I would say, "You don't get week two until it's unlocked." Well, sure enough, there was nothing in week 2. Every week, I was popping something new in and doing live calls. As I did my live training, that became my product, so then the next series of events, the next time I went to promote it, now I had a full product already ready and all ready to be done. This is one of the best ways to productize a program or a product or a service that you may have when you're not even ready for it.

Productization #2

4 Week Video Series

Next strategy is to create a video series. Do a 4-week video series or a webinar series that you market for, and you say,"I'm going to give ..." You get your topic, and so the topics I'm going to cover. Instead of going deep-dish or entrée on one and hors d'oeuvres sample platter on the others, you actually go deep in every single one.

You do a 1 hour to 2-hour workshop, or live workshop using either a Google Hangout or Zoom. You could use webinars or teleseminars. I highly recommend these days now using platforms like Webinar Jam, and you can get our Webinar Jam link using Google Hangout, they are very simple, posting them on a webinar hangout page that you can find with ClickFunnels or use a live feed like Zoom.

https://unstoppablefamily.com/clickfunnels

https://unstoppablefamily.com/webinarjam

You do these, and you go deep in every one of them. Now, you're providing full value upfront, a constant value which is how we build a better audience in the first place, it's constantly adding value, adding value. I call it value, value offer, the VVO method. You give high value. You're inviting the world to join you, and you are now bringing them to a free workshop where you give it all, and in each segment, you give it all to them. Now they're getting free value, and you're developing your product. Once you do this four weeks, all of your 4 or 5 hot points that you can teach on, then you go back, you go to ClickFunnels, you create a membership site, and you put your products in there.

Then, your next step is to do a webinar that is more of the branded system style webinar where you're offering again. Your entrée first, sampling the other four topics, like your speak-to-sell talk, your webinar talk, where you're giving them an example of what you do, and you go deep in one. You teach for the first 45 minutes. You sample for 15 minutes, and then you make your offer. Now, you're able to sell a program or a workshop with a product you just created by giving away value, because only live people get to have access to it, and now you have a program, and you have a webinar to sell that workshop or to sell that program. These are 2 of the best possible ways to productize a product or service that you don't have ready or you don't have prepared.

So now you have a high-value brand and a high-value product, now the exciting part is to monetize them and then automate so that you can join us on the beach with a cocktail!

3 Monetize

Monetizing is the area where everyone wants to find out how they can continue to take, let's say, a product or a service or a program, and package it up, and make more money from the one piece of content that they have. Monetizing your creations. Most people tend to have so much content. In fact, I'm a content ... I don't want to say "whore," but I want to say "content whore." I'm content-heavy. I'm a content monster, whatever you want to call it. I consistently create new and more content. I take one cat and try to skin six different ways. One thing that we find is that most people, they're not usually out of content. They're just out of monetizing. They constantly keep creating more content so they can sell new stuff. Instead, you need to take the current content that you've got, and repackage it, or bundle it up, into a new look, or a new type of program that you can sell. This way, you're not only attracting a new customer, but you're attracting a different eyeball. Someone that may have overlooked your program before is now open and willing to invest in you and more importantly in themselves.

People that have physical products can do very similar things. Package it differently ... Let's say it's an outfit or clothing company. Package up a full outfit. Make products that specifically pertain to women, or relate to men. Remember, stay focused on who your target audience is, just add a twist. Monetizing is something that can be done in stand-up stage talks, or speak-to-sell talks, webinars, consistently in events, and on your website, in your checkout process. My personal favorite way to monetize, in the online digital world is by creating a free value-based webinar with a catchy awesome headline and a tagline, giving them exactly what you're going to sell or offer to them, or teach them actually, and then you create an automated sales funnel. We're going to go into automation in a moment.

One Time Offer

Earlier I taught you about creating a webinar or a video series. So now you invite your target audience to your webinar. You place an ad on Facebook; you send it to your email list, or you post it up on a video. Invite them to come and join you. "I'm going to teach you five different ways to X, Y, and Z." They register for this webinar by an automated registration and then what happens when they register, it goes to a Thank You page. On this Thank You page, you place a one-time offer, an OTO they call it, where it says, "Thank you. You registered for our webinar. I'm really excited to have you there." But wait, before you go, I want to get you started. I want to make sure you're able to monetize, or you're able to learn before the webinar gets going, and begin to apply my teachings to your business right now." Place this text below. "This is just a one-time offer I'm going to give you. I normally sell this for $197." Always give the value, and then you give the one-time offer just for them. "For those of you that are here today and are registered, I'm going to give it to you for $7."

This is now called monetization. Where every lead, especially if you're paying for marketing, every lead is worth something. Now you have a lead that maybe cost you $3 to acquire, and then you sell them a one-time offer for $7, that lead not only paid for itself but now you've made money on it. Whether they buy or not, your products, your program, you've made up your dollars in the promotion. This then creates a buyers list. This buyers list now becomes all of your future promotions, whether they come to your webinar or not, you've now monetized that marketing campaign. That's one of the absolute best.

Email Follow-Up

Next is, through email. You might be building a list on your blog. You may be building your list for your webinars. Maybe they overlooked that one-time offer, but now you create an email backend, which has a sequence of, value, value, value, offer. Then you give them that one-time offer again, but you rephrase it. You repackage it. You position it a bit differently, and the price goes up. Remember the first time? That same product was only $7. Now you double the price. You put that into your email sequence. You write and give them a transformation that they will get for buying that program or that product from you. We always call it selling the destination and not the plane. People want to buy the destination. What they're going to get, the transformation they're going to get, from buying your product or your program. Now, in your emails, you're selling the destination, and you're giving them that one-time offer to buy your product or your program. That's another powerful way to monetize, whether you have a physical product, a book, or you have a digital product.

Bundling Your Products/Other People's Products

Next strategy for monetization is packaging it up and bundling it up with other products. Now, you have a product you've already created; maybe you do a webinar, so you've created a bit more content. Now you package it up and give them the lot. So you either can go a la carte and buy one program, or they get everything at a discounted price below the individual value base of that product. Now you can take a product you've already created or workshop, and then add on. It could be someone's else's product. You could buy a private label right (PLR) to someone's product, and sell that along with yours. Now, they're not only getting yours, but they're getting someone else's because you do a joint venture, or you buy the private label rights, and you productize it with someone else's. Using private label rights is one of the most powerful ways to monetize or to create a product. Relabel it yourself and make it your own product. You can use that as a giveaway. You can use that as a free 'Tripwire,' they call it, where you're giving them a product. It's one of the best ways to bundle up and continue to monetize.

JVs

Joint ventures are another incredible way for you to monetize your value and what you offer to the marketplace. A joint venture is you partnering up with someone else, and either doing the webinar for their list, or they come to your list, and they offer their product to your service, and you split the commissions. This works the best with one-off products that are under $500 typically, or $1000 because you go to someone else's list. Maybe it's a workshop. If it's a skill or a marketing skill that you have, or maybe it's a relationship coach, and someone has written a book, and they've got a major list of men and women in their group. You can make your pitch to their list, and you share the revenue profit. You always want to be sure that you're doing this and it makes sense. That it's profitable enough for you to do this JV. If you're the one doing all the work, let's say you're charging $600 for a 4-week workshop, and you are doing all the work, and you split the profits, you're only making less than $75 for every workshop that you do. I want to make sure we're always valuing ourselves, and that our JVs make sense.

One-off products work really nicely if you're not doing a lot of manual work at a lower price point, but your workshops are going to be a specialty to help someone make money and build their business. It can be anywhere from $997 to $1497, and then you can split the profits with your JV. 50-50 is typically one of the best points and percentages to share your profits with your JV partners. You can also do this with events where you bring someone into your event. You ask them to come and speak and allow them to sell their products or their services, and you make a percentage of what you have to offer. This is one of the best ways to monetize more of what you do and to get your name and your brand in front of more people.

As mentioned previously our next strategy for monetizing is hosting a live webinar or a show every single week that is pure value-based. Where you are doing a value-based, whatever your topic is, and you're giving it away for free. You create, either a live broadcast page or a Google Hangout page. ClickFunnels is one of the best. They have what's called the webinar sales funnel that you can use and turn it into an automated funnel. What it does, it allows you to have a live broadcast page all the time, and on that live broadcast page, you have buttons, and you have offered. Now, you're monetizing your value-based proposal without selling. Not everyone wants to be sold to, but if you have a webinar that allows you to share your value and give them free content and free value all the time ... On the right-hand side, you might have a button that says, "Access My Free Download." Let's say you give them an e-book on that free download. Inside of it is loaded full of links to your products. If you like this, you want more of this. You can say "Go here to find more." Or go, "To go get deeper into this subject, go here." Takes you to your product page. On the right-hand side of that live broad-cast page, you can also do an offer. You can have an event.

So now you're productizing, and you're monetizing every-thing while you're giving value. This is when I call, it's the value, value, offer. This is the way to build the 7-figure list that keeps people totally in your space, and you're not always selling to them. It makes your customers want to keep coming back for more because of what you're giving them. When they're ready to buy, they will buy. This is a powerful midway to monetize your value and your time, all of the time.

Then of course, when you have an automatic funnel, it sends an email for the replays. Gives you those offers again, and it keeps people coming back. The email send, "Hey, if you didn't get the live show offer, make sure you grab it here." Now, you're constantly giving stuff to people, and you're giving them value all the time, and they end up wanting to buy from you. This is a powerful way to monetize your value-based content without selling all the time.

4 Automation

Creating and running your own business can be both fun and fulfilling, but it can also take up a lot of your time and energy to make it a success.

However, when you take your business online you immediately give yourself the ability to automate it to a degree never seen before in conventional businesses.

Many online businesses can be almost entirely automated. Sure, they take a good business mindset and plenty of time and effort before you'll see good results. They'll also require at least a little ongoing maintenance to keep them going.

I'm not going to tell you that setting up or running an internet business is quick and effortless, but I am going to tell you that if you set up your business, correctly you can utilize the power of automation and free up large chunks of your valuable time.

A few things you need to automate:

Online Pages Hosting System like Clickfunnels http://unstoppablefamily.com/clickfunnels

- Opt-in page - where your reader/prospect puts in their name and email in return for something of value
- Bridge/thank you page
- Sales Page or Offer Page
- Email Sequence for non-buyers and buyers

Selling Products

With your website and online sales letter you can sell 24 hours a day to an international audience, that's a lot of potential customers, in a lot of different time zones. You may have heard of the saying ‘Make money while you sleep’, or in Brian’s case while you surf!

Don't worry, though; your website can do the selling and take orders for you, again even while you sleep. You won't need to stay awake all day and night to do it yourself. We use Click Funnels for all our membership sites, and sales pages to promote our products and services. Inside the system, my emails work for me, so I don't have a to.

Oh and if you don't even fancy the effort of making a product you can always be an affiliate of someone else's product, I did it for the first eight years of working online, but always be sure your values match what you are selling, or you can ruin your hard earned brand reputation overnight.

Taking Payment

Having your website being your 24-hour international salesman is awesome, but you don't want people phoning you up 24 hours a day to make their payments.

Product Delivery

So if you're planning to wake up in the morning, count the money you earned while you slept and then spend your morning shipping products, I'm about to disappoint you.

You'll have to think of another way to spend your morning because you're now selling downloadable information products, audio, video, eBooks, etc. This means that not only did your website make the sales and take the payments, it already delivered the products to your customers.

Customer Services

Let's start by pointing out that your customers are likely to be extremely happy by now. With waiting around for postmen or driving to the depot to pick up parcels that couldn't be delivered.

The product was delivered to them immediately after their purchase. People nowadays are more impatient than ever so they'll be very impressed with your superfast delivery.

That's a great start to keeping your customers happy, but if you want to further reduce your customer queries by a significant amount, use a FAQ or knowledge base. They really work and can automate the answering of the vast majority of your customer's questions.

Staying in Contact

You can automate your customer follow ups too with an email list management service. With automated subscribing, unsubscribing and good use of auto-responders, you can sell more products to new or existing customers and automate much of this process too.

Also, with social networking tools like Twitter you can use auto follow tools and message scheduling to reach new or existing customers, again being largely automated.

Almost Everything Else

So, having automated most of your business you'd expect us to be done now, leaving you with just the tasks that can't be automated?

Well, we're not quite done yet. That's where we introduce virtual assistants. Although not technically automation, if the remaining tasks you don't enjoy doing are done for you, that's as good as automation from our point of view.

What remains after all this is one last problem to solve, what do you do with your free mornings now you don't need to be selling, taking payments, shipping and answering customer queries?

It's entirely up to you what you spend your newly freed up time doing. From a business mindset perspective, I'd recommend being the visionary for your business, the entrepreneur, the content creator and the master marketer. These are all tasks I wouldn't want to outsource completely. More on outsourcing in a later chapter.

The key point here is not what you do with your newly found freedom; it's the fact that with the help of internet business and automation you've freed up your time in the first place, so you can spend it doing whatever you really enjoy doing.

Jodi Harman – The 'Forever Girlfriend'

"Within a few short weeks of working with Rhonda, I have been able to take all my plans out of my head and create the perfect online business model with automation so I don't have to work so hard"

I am so glad I met Rhonda Swan! I knew I wanted to create an online program with videos and a sales process to make it all automated but I had no idea how to structure it, do the automation or even what a sales funnel was. When Rhonda and I spoke and she described what she does and how she helps people become freedom-preneurs with systems and automation, I knew I needed her. Within a few short weeks of working with Rhonda I have been able to take all my plans out of my head and create the perfect online business model with automation so I do not have to work so hard. She has an amazing team that helps when I am stuck, and her brilliant mind of walking prospects through a sales process was just what I needed to launch and explode my business.

I have spent $10K+ with other companies and wished I had found Rhonda first. Rhonda has been true to her "sealed with a kiss promise" and continues to deliver over and over new ideas to implement for more sales in my new system. Some of my branding was already completed when we met but Rhonda helped me narrow down my niche market and focus my message directly to the audience. Refining and defining my brand has made all the difference.

Thank you Rhonda!

Jodi Harman ~ The Forever Girlfriend

The "Unstoppable Family" Secrets To Living As A Freedom-Preneur

When we coined the term freedom-preneur in, 2011 it caught a buzz almost instantly. **Freedom** being the operative word in Freedom-Preneur? Since freedom has so many meanings to people, when we talk about freedom we are focused on being able to do what you want when you want with who you want and where you want. As I like to say, having freedom is about living a life of bells and whistles vs being focused on having them. Since the word want is used so often, freedom is of course about knowing what it is that you really want. So many of us are going after what we think we should want and our wants are blind and ambitious. As the Unstoppable Family we know that the reason we have had the success in living the free life that we have, has come from knowing what we want. Defining this in a term that others could relate to is where freedom-preneur was born and now we want you to fully understand and embody the power of it!

Entrepreneurs are known for being in business, sharing their techniques and secrets of building a business before others know how.

A freedom-preneur is about being free and before others know how to do it...are you getting this so far? Why would we have a business for if not the idea of freedom?

Too often we forget the ends and get caught in the means as if it is set in stone that this one way we learned is the only way to have what we want. We are here to defy that idea so that the focus is your freedom and not the business aspect. The Preneur side is important, but don't worry, it will come. In becoming a freedom preneur you must know what you want to do, where you want to do it and when you want to do it.

This is your *life* we are talking about and despite popular belief, your life is not a business.

What do you really want to do?

What are your passions and your gifts?

Where would you like to live that passion out? What country, setting or at least type of weather? Who do you want to be around? What times of day do you want to be doing what?

I know that these are very different questions we ask than when we are just starting a business and that is what makes being a freedom-preneur so powerful. When you know what you want and you are exploring the many ways to experience it, your service that will render your income is a natural factor that emerges! Read on to see more comparing factors to understand why you want to be a master of embracing freedom vs business!

Please answer the above questions and take the time to

research options! Your dream journey is but a few barriers and beliefs being broken down, away.

Making a Business or Making a Life

Most of the time when we think of someone that is an entrepreneur we think of someone who is good at making a business. When something happens in the economy or in the world they are the first to find a way to monetize that very happening. This is a great ability as often times they are fulfilling a need, yet this does not consider the full scope of life, especially an inherently free one. When the real estate market went up entrepreneurial people became real estate investors and they developed a million and one ways to capitalize on the up market. The thing about this though, is that most of them did not consider making a life and their work kept them exactly where the market was in regards to location. The next occurrence is that they were not living a passion and it was not something that was a natural reoccurring part of their life and the lives of others.

A market that went up had to come down and quite of few investor related businesses found themselves searching for something to merely sustain a lifestyle and unfortunately many fell short. Subsequently, as the market crashed, so did their bank accounts and for many of them their freedom as well. In your current opinion of freedom and what it means to you, did they actually ever have freedom?

Right now,

before you read on, why don't you go ahead and define freedom to you. What does it mean and what does it look like? How do you think it must be obtained and what are the "rules to the game", if you will?

As a Freedom-Preneur you are going to make a life. You know that freedom is about just that, freedom. If you were making a life and money was not an issue, or at least you did not believe that you needed a large surplus of money first, in order to do it, what would you do? Now there is no need to be in a hurry, answer that question before you move on... The idea that you will be a good businessperson and then have freedom is just that, an idea. There is no trade off of now for later and the number of entrepreneurs who are focused on solely money making activities that make it to the white sandy beaches of retirement are unfortunately far and few between. We want you to focus on making a life. Why do you have to have a bunch of money in the bank in order to live the life of your dreams?

You don't! If you love what you do, why would you do something for 40 years just to never have to do it again? You would not! As a Freedom-Preneur, you know how to navigate your life and the world, you bring your passions to become profits and you know that you can learn to do anything at any time and find a new "way" in the wide open world that we have at our fingertips! Make a life and a living will follow and if you focus on making a living, you might find that you don't have much of a life outside of networking meetings and business brunches.

Name your top 5 Passions.

List 5 ways you can make money online.

What are 5 careers you think you could not do and why, not would not, could not do.

Can Money Buy you Freedom?

Ok, so how many of us have heard the term, "do you own your business or does your business own you?" There are many reasons that this ends up being the case for so many aspiring entrepreneurs. One is that we don't know other market factors that may affect our business that end up having our projected profits not quite meet what we are receiving in reality. Another reason is that your life situation where you run your business is so expensive that it seems almost impossible to get ahead and the more you make the more you find yourself spending to impress the next echelon of clients you hope to attract and "WOW". One of the biggest reasons is that we choose businesses that sound fun without really thinking it through and what we are doing is not mostly full of activities that we love and make our hearts sing.

Have you done any of these three things?

1. Had a business fail because the profits were affected by unforeseen market conditions?
2. Spent more money right alongside making it and never got "ahead"?
3. Burnt out and felt uninspired so you did not do what it "took" to go from good to great?

If this all sounds a bit too familiar, that is precisely why you want to look into the life of a Freedom-Preneur. You see, a freedom-focused individual finds a life that encompasses much of what they love so they find themselves completing the work that they do from a place of inspiration. A pioneer of freedom also understands the many elements of freedom and considers where they want to be and what they really need to spend, they don't follow the norm. As a result, their lives tend to not always have so many ancillary costs that keep them buried in work and do things that make them happy with confidence and are not living life for someone else or under some false illusion of success that might not be as tried and true as we think!

What do you think it takes to be successful?

How much does your life cost you per month?
Have you ever considered a new environment that might have you living healthier and happier for half the price, or less?
Do you think of your passions and see them as hobbies vs helpful?
How many things do you pay for each month that are for other people's benefit?

When was the last time you took a vacation?If you could go anywhere in the world right now, where would you go and why haven't you yet?

Consideration is not just Money

So many of us are caught in this idea that we need to make as much money as we can. The picture that most of us have painted of success goes something like this:

Make a bunch of money and live a lifestyle that is very luxurious and as we do this, our wealth continues to grow. As that wealth grows we will set up varying investments and we will accumulate enough money so that at some point, hopefully earlier than later, we will have enough to retire and not have to do anything for the rest of our lives. The only thing we then end up considering is how much we can make and how much that money we make can make us.

Have you actually thought this through?
Do you know how much money you would need?Have you mapped out something that you believe in, which will get you there despite varying markets?If you have, did you consider your happiness and well-being on the way there?
How many vacations are planned?
How many stamps will your passport have?
Do you really want to NEVER do anything again at some point, what does that even mean?
Is there a true picture of this retirement that is well thought out and digested?

This is all good and fine, yet I just don't personally know all that many people that have had this lifestyle work for them and it has been said many times that we will wear our best years out on the way to this phantom finale that may elude us. I can tell you that I love helping others and connecting, and I will never want to stop doing that. In the event that I did, I would want to learn something else and find a way to connect and contribute as it is an innate human behavior.

Most people who are in the delusion of this retirement game do not connect fully to the reality of the choices that they are making. Get your head out of the clouds and your feet on the ground and get real about what it will take and if it would be worth the ride if there was another option. Not only are we not guaranteed our later years, but we never know what financial markets hold either. One thing that you do have for certain, if you choose to, is your gift and the ability to navigate the world and live amongst the fine people in it. When you know you have options you know you will have a life.

In 2000, Argentina pegged their peso to the dollar and then it crashed leaving everyone who had money in the bank without money. There was NO money! NONE! What if you had worked your whole life to 55 and this happened?

I know we think we are exempt from these sort of things in America yet the crash that began in 06'/07' has caused at least an 8 TRILLION dollar loss of wealth to American people. By no means are we wanting to scare anyone, we are just challenging you to look at what is for certain and maybe re-evaluate some perspectives and priorities.

How much would it cost you to retire? Do you know how to navigate a foreign country without the use of planes and hotels.com? Can you name one country where you can live without being a citizen? Have you ever acquired an entry visa, and we are not talking credit cards? Is Thailand a Democracy, Monarch or Communist Country?

We live in a world and the world has options for us if we know that it does. It is not our fault that we don't know, unless we know that we can! I am officially telling you that there are options and knowing them, whether you indulge or not, will give you piece of mind at a minimum. I know for certain that I can find a place to live and offer my talents in some form, so that no matter what, my family can be cared for. That, to me, is a Freedom-preneur at its finest. I know that I can travel to most countries in the world and I know how to find entry and exit requirements, all forms of transportation, rules on how easy or difficult it is to stay there, work visas and transportation to and around and that allows me to feel comfortable and experience amazing things I once only dreamed of. Would you like the same for your life?

Write down 5 countries that interest you and research their entry policy. Find at least three means of traveling around. Find out if you can work there.

Find out the price for a rental to live there Research a bit of the political history and cultural history.

We look at Consideration in a different way than money, we look at it as a verb vs a noun. Consideration is to consider many things and in the eyes of a true freedom-preneur, money is just one of the many things. We consider being happy, the effects of not having parents around for the children that we are raising, the environment, other places where we might be able to have our cake and eat it too and how to do something that we thoroughly enjoy. If you are a super star freedom-preneur you also consider that what you do makes a big difference in the lives of others as we believe that each and every human being has a calling and something to offer that enhances the lives of others genuinely and hurts no one, something that we call mutual interest.

The other factor of consideration is making it equitable. What if you could do something that seems hard to enter because it is so competitive and high paying, yet you could do it for what was equitable? If your life only cost $3000/mo in order for it to be spectacular beyond your wildest dreams, would you need to demand your "worth" or could you find a win-win? Options are awesome aren't they?!

Next time you think of what consideration is, make it an action and apply it to your own life and the lives of those around you and you will find the payouts have dividends that deliver! Consider you. Consider your family. Consider the now and you will find an answer that glitters far more than gold! We know that you need money to live but it does not have to be a now and then...and you might not need as much of it as you think you do to have the paradise life that you dream of!

Options are Abundant for those who know what they want and know they can have it

I know that we talk about knowing what you want a lot and we can't help but emphasize just how important it is. Many leaders of success and positive social change have said that there is nothing that can get between someone who knows what they want and the fruition of that very thing and that is because when we acknowledge that we really want something we acknowledge that it is possible.

What would you want if time and money were not an issue? What do you feel obligated to?What do you think you have to do?Inventory your beliefs.

What are you attached to and what conditions have you placed on your success? Who are you trying to make happy or who do you fear letting down? Evaluate your relationships ... if you want acceptance is it coming from a place of giving? Are your relationships based on mutual interest, meaning that you consider them and that you consider you?

How many things a day do you do out of fear?

In the world that we live in many of us have not learned yet to ask ourselves what we want sans the demands of what society has told us we had to do in order to get it. We tell ourselves that we want to do things but if we are to peel back the layers of it, most of the things that we think we want we don't actually want, we have just associated getting the thing we really want with getting those other things. For example, if you want to travel the world but you think you need a bunch of money to do it, you may say that you want to make as much money as you can, but if you knew that you could do it right now with the money that you had and that you could easily make more than enough to live on the road, that just might change your priorities. One of the best lessons I was ever given was to look at the things that I was doing on a daily, weekly, monthly and yearly basis and replace all have to's with want to's. If I could not find one, a want that is, I would have to find what I thought was the benefit of doing that thing. After doing this I had to research and see if there was anyone who had achieved what I wanted without taking the steps that I thought I "had to" in order to get there. What I found was that each and every thing that I thought I had to do was just that, a thought. I am going to suggest that you do exactly the same thing, and do it now, you matter enough to take the time! There are rules we must follow as far as legalities but last time I checked there was no law that said you can't have your dreams until you save up enough money to retire! If you are living by that rule than you are a simple shift in perspective and priority away from having the life that you want now, and *that* is key in being an Unstoppable Freedom-preneur.

Making a difference or Making Money?

So many of us are under the impression that those who make a difference are those that have the most money. We are told that we are to make a bunch of money and then we can donate that money to a cause. You always hear about the rich and famous who are helping with foundations or adopting needy children from around the globe, yet you too can make just as much of a difference as any millionaire mogul and you can do it right now!

How would you like to impact the world? Who are your favorite famous figures who contribute?

Do you know five ways that you could give back and make it part of your life?

Have you considered encompassing giving back into your business?

One of the best ways to make a great living is to build "making a difference" right into what you are doing. Tom's did it with the Abrogado shoes and we are doing it with "Educate yourself, Educate a child", in both cases when products are purchased, money and "goods" immediately goes to benefiting children. This is not the limit to it though! Nope, not at all. Your business can involve the improvement of something. You could work for an NGO or start one that would fund your life. You can teach English in societies where children need to learn English to increase the probability of finding a job that will allow them to support their family!

List 5 gifts that you can give to the world.

List 5 businesses that inherently make the world better without causing harm.

When you make a difference, money seems to flow to you effortlessly and making a difference is really what we are all here to do and want to do at our core. We have spent a large amount of our adult lives traveling and have spent most of the last 4 years living all over the world and if there is one thing that is ubiquitously consistent, it is the desire to serve and help our fellow man/woman. No matter where you go, even the sourest of people light up with joy at the opportunity to genuinely help another.

Recall at least five cases when someone you thought was not kind, surprised you.

Recall at least five instances where someone you judged had an experience you could not imagine having gone through it, then imagine it.

When we focus on only making money we miss out on the joy of giving and we can lose touch with who we really are and what reality is in the *world* that we live in. Making a difference can be part of your business model like when you empower others to go and live the life that makes their heart sing! Making a difference is when you give back to those in need, which is everyone, as a part of your product and making a difference can be your way of life!

An Entrepreneur makes money and then makes a life. A Freedom-Preneur makes a life and that is where they make their money so they don't live with the weight of crossing their fingers ambitiously hoping for the nightmare of the concrete jungle to one day end and wake up to their dram, they live it right now!

Freedom-Preneurs make a difference as a part of making money, not as a latter by-product. They also know that there is more than one way to "skin a cat" and know how to live a free life in many settings and ways.

They consider many things with a balanced awareness of themselves, others and the world and they know the price on freedom is just a mindset away, not a million or two(dollars that is) ! Are you ready to trade in your outdated "outfit" of life for something that speaks to your own spectacular style and way?

You do have to make your own music and sing your own special song ... so get singing as a Freedom-Preneur and while you are at it, take a friend or two with you! Surfing waves and drinking cold cerveza is always more fun in groups anyhow!

Unstoppable Action Steps

Who is my 'sexiest' customer, client or audience?

____

____

____

What does my sexiest customer desire or what problem do they need to solve?

____

____

____

What is my product or service USP?

____

____

____

We have sooooo many FREE resources to help you develop your sexy Brand on our FREE bonus page below.

https://unstoppablemomma.com/bonus for your FREE book resources to help you.

Horacio Gallegos 'With Great Mentors You Can Live Your Dreams!'

"When the student is ready the teacher will appear. For me that teacher was Rhonda Swan"

They say that when the student is ready the teacher will appear. For me, that teacher and mentor was Rhonda Swan. About 4 years ago, I was going through some major changes in my life and I was ready and hungry for a new career and lifestyle. I had gone through some challenging times in the real estate industry, and had finally broken through to some moderate success. But I knew I wanted something different this time. I had a new vision for my life, but I had absolutely no idea how I was going to get there.

It is at this time that Rhonda and her family came into my life through a social media connection. I saw how Rhonda and Brian had managed to create a dream lifestyle while traveling and working from their laptops, and I instantly knew that the Universe had delivered the person that would guide me through this amazing new world. She accepted to mentor me, and my life has never been the same since. Rhonda not only taught me the most cutting edge internet and video marketing skills, but has instilled in me, through her own example, and new type of work ethic, positivity, and servant's heart that I did not even know I possessed. She has supported me in all of my endeavors since we first met, and I can honestly say that I do not know a more intelligent, hard-working, and loyal person on this planet. I owe a huge part of my success as a digital marketing consultant to her.

Horacio Gallegos

17

Branding YOU!

Nicky Jones *Branding You!*

"I went from being unemployed, illness and depression to now being the proud owner of my own online business and as happy as I could ever have imagined."

My journey with Rhonda Swan and the Unstoppable Family has been a life changing experience and continues to be so. A few years ago, you could say I was at the lowest point of my life. I was suffering from illness and depression and was desperate to find something to get me out of the dark place that I was in. I searched online for something I could do that would give me the freedom to work from home and ultimately my laptop. After searching many options, I was put in contact with The Unstoppable Momma, Rhonda Swan and the amazing Unstoppable Tribe of people she works directly with to empower and inspire.

I was blown away by the amount of support and attention I was given to help me develop my own personal brand based on my passion and skill set. Not only was I given consistent one on one advice and help, but Rhonda has brought together an amazing group of people who are all willing to give and give unconditionally. The Unstoppable Tribe and Freedom-Preneur Academy is networking on another level!

When I first started attending the mastermind events, hosted by Rhonda Swan, I knew next to nothing about the online business world. After the first event, I attended, I walked away with a crystal clear working plan of activities with the knowledge on how to make it successful online. I could never have hoped to have found a better mentor. A person who is truly invested in making a difference in my life and helping me establish a successful business and opening so many doors of opportunity for myself within business, through her personal mentorship, the creation of The Unstoppable Tribe and the development of The Freedom-Preneur Academy.

I can honestly say the continued wealth of infor-mation and support I and many others have received from Rhonda Swan has changed my life completely. I went from being in an appalling place to being in the best position I have ever been in life and business. I went from being unemployed, illness and depression to now being the proud owner of my own online business and as happy as I could ever have imagined. I now have not one but two successful business websites centered around human consciousness, spirituality, self-empowerment, myst-icism, personal development and healing as an Intuitive Life and Business Consultant.

I now have the ability to offer various workshops, online and in person, one on one consultations as well as providing free information on these sites and social media. I have an online presence as a public figure which has given me the opportunity to travel the world and become an International Public Speaker. And most recently, a budding author. I can whole heartedly say none of this would have been possible without Rhonda Swan and her creation of The Unstoppable Family and Tribe and the Freedom-Preneur Academy. Thank you, Rhonda, for giving me the tools to change my life to one of happiness and abundance in all areas of my life!

Nicky Jones

Founder/Facilitator of Lifestyle Alchemy

www.lifestyle-alchemy.com

www.nickyjones.com.au

Personal branding: a puzzle only a few have solved and the world is waiting for your personal brand to be shared. We have seen icons like Jay-Z, JLo Oprah Winfrey, and the Kardashians create global brands that span across industries. From books to shows to endorsement deals, these personalities have built multi-billion dollar empires by their names alone. Although these examples are exclusive to the entertainment realm, there are many other examples such as Melinda Gates, Malala, J.K. Rowling and Martha Stewart that we can identify. What are some of the standard components of having a solid personal brand? A successful personal brand has multiple must-haves that include:

- Being an expert in your industry
- Books and publications
- Working with media
- Corporate clients and sponsorships
- And more recently, developing a solid digital media platform

As an entrepreneur or young professional, social media is the component to begin to focus on.

Kim Kardashian has been an expert, harnessing social media and using it to create relationships with her fans, communicate with media, secure corporate sponsor-ships and self-publish and self-promote her products. What you must keep in mind is that simply creating accounts on social media sites and pushing out your content is not going to help grow your brand. You must have a concrete plan that encompasses various tools and channels simultaneously while sharing a consistent message.

With brands, people expect consistency. Imagine walking into Zara and seeing sleek European style pieces replaced with tacky, ill-fitting clothes. You would walk right out because that's not what you went there for or what you have come to associate with the name Zara. A brand promises a certain level of quality. They tell a story. The same goes for your personal brand.

Brand consistency is divided into two parts:

Tangibles and Intangibles

Tangibles relate to the things you can see and touch. This is also what people tend to focus on most. It's your logo, website, graphics, color scheme, etc.

The intangibles however, are just as, if not more important. The brand personality and brand story guide the creation of those tangible items. They set the tone for the look and feel of your brand. Today it is more important than ever for people to see the person behind the brand, to connect with their story, their vulnerability and to be seen as 'just like me'.

What's the singular driving force behind the success of unusual entrepreneurs like Steve Jobs, Richard Branson, Bill Gates, Oprah Winfrey, Donald Trump, and many others in their league?

Is it their ground breaking innovations or exceptional business skills or determination?

The answer is neither.

While it's obvious that all of these attributes definitely contributed to their success, as a matter of fact, these are the very attributes that have been often popularized. The truth is that there's something more subtle that's been frequently overlooked but is highly responsible for the success stories of most unusual entrepreneurs.

What's this often overlooked secret weapon?

Their Personal Brands

What Is Personal Branding?

Personal branding is the way you as an entrepreneur differentiate yourself from the rest of your industry so that you can really stand out from the crowd. You do this by articulating your uniqueness, your unique value proposition, whether professional or personal, and then leveraging it across platforms with a consistent message and image to achieve a specific goal or outcome.

A well-executed personal branding campaign creates a strong, consistent, and specific association between the individual and the perceived value they offer.

What is the first thing you think of when you look at the picture of Marilyn Monroe?

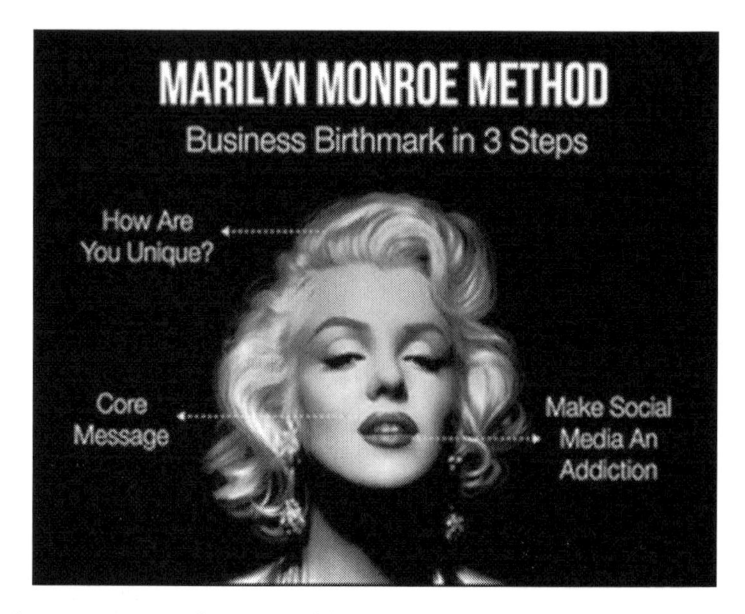

I'm sure most of you would say The Platinum Hair, Ruby Red Lips, or more noticeable, her birthmark. Marilyn's birthmark became her most distinguishable trait and landed her the most sought after actress in the 1960's. Good thing we don't have to be Marilyn to be noticed today or to create an identifiable brand in the eyes of our customers.

We need to make a statement and stick to our values using the 3 D's or Marilyn Monroe Method creating your business birthmark in 3 simple steps.

1. Determine what makes you unique or USP
2. Define Your Core Message and Values
3. Dominate Social Media

Known Personal Branded Entrepreneurs

Let's take some clues from the unusual entrepreneurs mentioned in the introduction.

Steve Jobs

Steve Jobs is known as a perfectionist. He had a passion for design. He understood what a personal brand is about. It is your unique essence and impact in the world. Steve reminded us to pursue our uniqueness. His personal brand defined all his actions. It was about the relentless pursuit of excellence. It was about innovating, not being afraid to break the rules to be different.

He didn't care about making money. He cared about something bigger. Your personal brand is always about something bigger. Here is Steve Jobs' famous question to John Sculley, former Apple CEO

> "Do you want to spend the rest of your life selling sugared water or do you want a chance to change the world?"

Richard Branson

Richard Branson, is clear about being a risk taker. He is not your typical CEO in a blue suit and white shirt. He is a dare devil who was dressed in a wedding gown when he launched Virgin Bridal, and was not dressed at all when he launched his book, Virginity. Among his first big risky ventures was signing the Sex Pistols onto his record label when no one else would even consider them.

Since then, he has taken on both British Airways with Virgin Airlines and Coke, the strongest brand in the world, with

Virgin Cola. Even outside of the professional arena, Richard Branson is clear about being a risk-taker. While many CEOs travel the world comfortably in their plush corporate jets, Richard Branson decided he was going to circumnavigate the world in a hot air balloon.

Oprah Winfrey

Oprah Winfrey is the human brand of show biz. Oprah's personal brand is associated with celebrity, charity, education and successful launches of products. She cares for people and is willing to share of herself to help people advance. This clarity about what makes her unique is consistent among all of her endeavors. And it is constantly visible to her target audience through her numerous ways of interacting with the public.

Oprah's business success is built solidly on a powerful personal brand marketing strategy. Oprah has turned her talents, skills and values into a multi-billion-dollar media empire that's still growing. Other media personalities have tried to emulate her personal brand strategy. So far, no one else has been able to match her ability to make women laugh, cry and dream about how to "live your best life."

The Brand Called YOU

"All of us need to understand the importance of branding. We are CEOs of our own companies: Me Inc. To be in business today, our most important job is to be head marketer for the brand called YOU."

– Tom Peters in Fast Company

Most entrepreneurs in their quest to build a business often forget to build themselves in the process. They focus on developing the image and reputation of their business and products/services and completely lose touch with their own image and reputation.

They erroneously believe that the only thing the market cares about is the products/services they offer or the businesses they create. In the end, they end up building a company without a human face.

The human factor is the most powerful factor of all factors of production. The most powerful brand on earth, is the brand called YOU!

People buy from people. Companies are built by people. Products are created by people. People connect with people, not products. The more of yourself you put out there, the more acceptable your products/services will become. When they have bought into your person, then they will buy into your company.

Successful entrepreneurs know this and that's why they inject themselves into the businesses they create. They literally become the face of their companies, putting themselves endlessly out there for the market to know, like and trust them.

7 Facts About Personal Branding

"Your brand is what people say about you when you're not in the room" – Jeff Bezos, Founder of Amazon

- You already have a personal brand whether you want one or not.
- Your personal brand is built 24/7 and 365 days per year through what you say, but even more importantly, through what you do.
- Personal branding is all about your Audience. Your personal brand exists in the minds of your Audience.
- Your personal brand exists in the minds of others in the way they perceive, think, and feel about you.
- The only way to have a strong personal brand is to carefully define it.
- The best personal brands are credible, so you must prove that you can deliver what you promise.

I have put together a workbook to go along with this really important part of your business, make sure you download your workbook on creating your own sexy brand from my book bonus page :-

https://unstoppablemomma.com/bonus

Here is an example of the beginning of your workbook - What Are Your Brand Colors Saying?

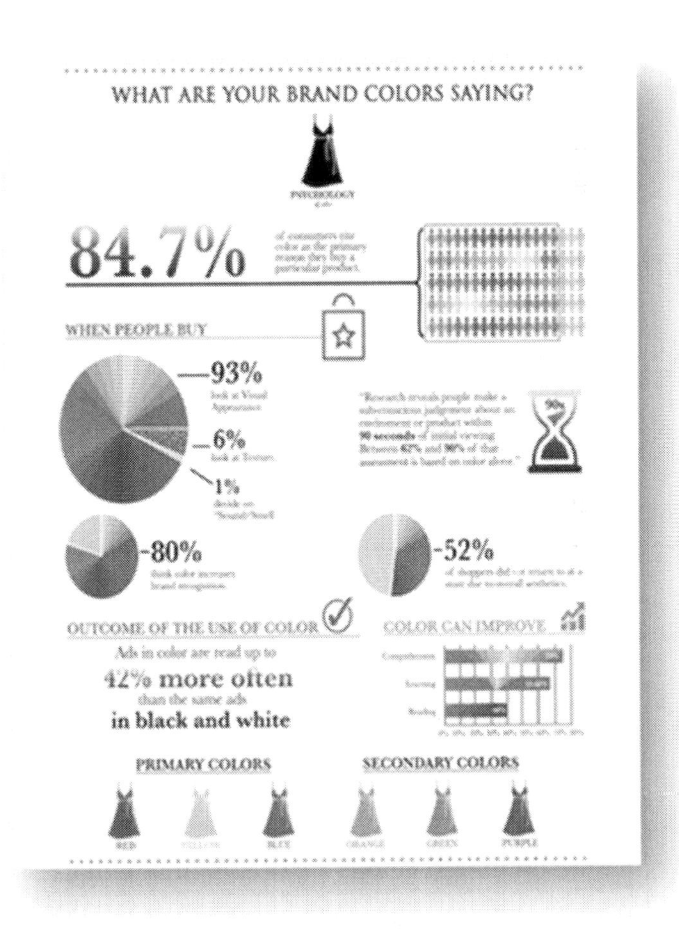

Bernie Martin Turn Yours Passions Into Profit

"We are all only one connection away from our lives changing dramatically. Don't be afraid to reach out to people that have what you want."

It was 5:45 am when my alarm went off; telling me it was time to get up. I began my daily ritual of hitting snooze for the first of 3 times as I looked through my Facebook newsfeed. After dragging myself out of bed I began my one-hour drive into work. For 2 years this was how my mornings started, even though I was my own boss.

I owned a dog daycare, which I had started from scratch and had built it into a fairly successful little business. I had done it ... I had been a dog trainer for a few years and had this vision of opening a dog daycare where I could teach dogs to socialize. I would take in dogs that weren't allowed at other daycares because they were too aggressive and work with them to learn how to socialize properly.

This was my vision ... but then everything changed.

I had a business partner at the time and this person's vision started to change as the dollar signs came in. I wanted to help dogs, my business partner wanted to make easy money and get rid of the problem dogs that actually needed the socialization.

The energy started to change at the daycare and my passion started to fade.

I remember the day like it was yesterday ... as I was scrolling through Facebook early one morning I came across a photo of a smiling family that called themselves The Unstoppable Family. I read their story of traveling the world and working online. I was intrigued.

I thought about The Unstoppable Family all day at work but kept telling myself there was no way it was possible for me to do what they were doing. The online world was foreign to me, I only knew how to work with my hands.

The next morning the same ad popped up and I ended up connecting with them ... the rest is a blur.

Within 3 months I had sold the dog day care in a search for really finding my passion. Over the course of the next 3 years I attended 6 events put on by Brian and Rhonda, which have changed my life dramatically.

They helped me focus on my passions and encouraged me to run with it.

My wife and I both changed career paths dramatically just because of that one Facebook ad from The Unstoppable Family. Ironically, I now run Facebook ads for other people and found my passion is helping other businesses grow.

My wife Tiffany who was also a dog trainer found her true passion was Craft Beer and has started a craft beer blog that has exploded over the last year.

I know Brian and Rhonda won't take the credit for what we have done but we have everything to thank them for. They would say they only told us to follow our passions and stick to them, we would say ... you told us to do it, and you showed us it was possible.

We are all only one connection away from our lives changing dramatically. Don't be afraid to reach out to people that have what you want.

Bernie Martin

18

Stay In Your Zone Of Genius

"Days are expensive.

When you spend a day you have one

less day to spend. So make sure you spend

each one wisely."

Jim Rohn

Sometimes You Just Need To Ask For Help

As an introduction to this chapter, I'd like to share our story about someone was and is such a big important part of our growth and our business – ***Jubril Agoro***.

Being an independent strong willed woman, I took on all of the roles of building our business myself. I would sit and learn for hours and hours all about marketing. Listening to webinars, to trainings, I bought products, I bought books, in fact Rich Dad Poor Dad started me off which lead me through a series of inspirational, personal development and marking books. I followed the 'gurus' and learned and modeled everything they did. And it came to a point where posting every day, writing blog posts every day, calling newspapers, back then I did 3 line newspaper ads looking at anything and everything as I walked down the street to see how I could get my information in front of more people, including creating coreplast plastic signs with the message that read 'Work from home, don't believe me don't call', I was just consumed.

But when we started to travel and my daughter was born, I had to start looking for someone who could be an expert. I of course waited until we were making enough money, then started to look into outsourcing. We had a guy that we had met back in 2005 in Whistler BC. His name was Jubril Agoro and we were in the same company together. He was 18 years old, and he was crunching it. He really understood how to market on eBay and YouTube and we became very close friends with him. We kind of lost touch until about 2009 when we reconnected with him. While we were traveling we had talked about hiring him to do our marketing. Anyway when we came back to Las Vegas in 2009 we met up with him. Little did we know, but he wasn't doing as well as we thought, and we were trying to puff up and act like we were really rocking it, but as you know we had just lost everything the year before.

So we get there and Jubril tells us he is staying at the El Cortez in downtown Las Vegas. Now we didn't know anything about the hotel but what was evident is that it wouldn't cost a lot of money to stay there, but that is the moment we created a lifelong business relationship and a partnership that lasted from 2009 until towards the end of 2015. For the whole of that time we were working together as partners and Jubril helped scale our business using YouTube and then FaceBook marketing, and he became Hanalei's Uncle Bril. But it started off with both of us starting off in such a low spot in our lives, this is the power of great relationships both in lives and in business, when you reach out to create partnerships, it's always great to reach out to find someone to work with.

However, partnerships are always very sensitive and we've been burned many times, but reaching out and knowing what your core competences are and knowing what you should outsource is vital. And finding someone that you can trust, and know very well to help you scale, is not only difficult to do but it is a blessing. And Jubril became such a huge part of our family, we've known him since he was 18 years old, we've gone through the highs the lows, the sads, the elations, the thousand, the millions and the o's of dollars, but all along we've travelled around the world together and all of us have grown and developed into incredible contributors to this world. And my little girl considers him as her uncle. It's interesting because Jubril was raised in the UK, his family is Nigerian, he was adopted by a white English family and he is charcoal black, 6 ft 4" and my daughter Hanalei always asked 'When am I going to be as tanned as Uncle Bril?' Because being raised a 3rd world child she's always been a minority, never seen black or white and she always wondered how she could be as tanned.

Developing relationships like this is absolutely vital to grow and scale your business. Starting this relationship in 2009 allowed us to free up our time and allowed us to travel. So just like Tim Ferris was teaching us to set up our system, have a ground o home base, which was Brian's family, we also then outsourced most of our marketing, and Jubril would travel around the world with us, shoot videos, and market together. This allowed us to scale, so when you are looking to create a freedom business you can't just do it all yourself, it is difficult and you do need to find a good team and understand outsourcing.

As you put each of the 4 key components of your sexy brand in place you will discover the downside of being an entrepreneur, or a solo-preneur and the main one is trying to everything yourself. You will find you are working so much IN your business you barely ever get time to work ON your business. You may start to lose sight of your vision, of your purpose and your mission. You simply CANNOT do everything yourself and the sooner you start building a team of people around you the faster your business will grow and the faster you will get your message out to a wider audience.

The first thing you need to ask yourself is 'which tasks do I do more than once?' The second is 'what is my zone of genius?' Quite simply anything else you do more than once, you create a system and then delegate to someone else to do, so you are able to concentrate on what you do best.

How to Give Your Customers Outstanding Value and Keep Your Sanity - OUTSOURCE

Your customers hire you to be the very person you are. They don't hire you to do things you can't do. If you can't spell, chances are your customers aren't looking for a proof-reader.

What you can do well is change the quality of your clients' lives using your life experience, brand, and expertise. If you waste your time trying to do simple chores that take your time away from caring for your clients and customers, you're not only losing money, but you're not serving them the way they need and want to be served. The answer is outsourcing, and we use it to be Unstoppable.

What is Outsourcing?

Outsourcing is a way of bringing the best quality to your clients without draining your own energies until you can't provide the secret sauce that is you. You simply find people who have the skills you need and hire them to fill in the gaps in your skills. You provide the passion; the Virtual Assistants you hire provide the skills. If you can't spell, you can outsource the spelling by hiring a proof-reader. If you're a great writer but you can't build a website, you hire someone who can make a quality website for you. If you need great artists to help your clients create their individual brands and logos, you hire terrific artists to do a fabulous job for you. If you have to create a product launch but don't have a clue how to build a sales funnel, the Virtual Assistants can step in and do the whole thing for you.

Most of the time, you can find people all over the world ready, able, and eager to help you. People from countries like the Philippines, where English is taught when they start school, will work for pennies on the dollar, which is very profitable for them. Our business was turned on its head when we were recommended to use Need a VA in the Philippines, run by our very dear friend and colleague, Jenny Jordan. It's one secret weapon that we use to enable us to work from anywhere in the world and still deliver fantastic services for our clients.

For more information you can contact Jenny here - www.unstoppablefamily.com/needava

Kimberley & Scott Vento From No Experience to Applying Skill That Will Last A Lifetime

"We learned how to tell our story in a captivating way that made people feel like they knew, liked and trusted us."

Rhonda and Brian are inspirational and gave us the mentorship we needed when we started our internet marketing business a few years ago. She taught us how to dig deep and find our core values to develop our own personal brand that would be recognized worldwide. We learned how to tell our story in a captivating way that made people feel like they knew, liked and trusted us. We developed the confidence in our ability to create a business through selling who we were and what we were passionate about doing rather than the products we sold.

My husband and I were able to take the skills we learned and apply them to different aspects of business, from internet marketing to real estate and took a year and a half off from our "normal" life to travel and live in Phuket, Thailand while running our business online.

We are so happy to have worked with Rhonda and Brian and the Unstoppable Family and our global community of FreedomPreneurs and we cherish the friendships we made with them that will outlast any products we will ever sell.

Kimberley & Scott Vento

Oceanside, CA

Inge Hart – *The Dutch Nomad Family*

"Let your work and business be part of your life, not the leading factor."

Starting up an online business without having been an entrepreneur before and no knowledge on the internet is challenging. We believe having a community, educational system and a coach to support you, will make the chances of succeeding bigger. That's why we joined the Freedom Preneur Movement and Academy and get coached by Rhonda Swan.

We didn't make that decision randomly. The Dutch Nomad Family lives by what we call the 5 pillars of a balanced life. Which basically means that every single day we make sure we have the feeling we had a balanced life by making sure we do our spiritual practice, exercise, eat healthy food, spend quality time with the kids and earn an income. What we gain from that is that our awareness is very high and we mentally and physically fit enough to take on a new challenge. Or as I like to put it, we are able to see and grab an opportunity at the right moment when they are presented to us.

So when we met Unstoppable Momma, Rhonda Swan, with her Unstoppable Family we knew quickly our lifestyle and view of life had similarities and their values overlapped ours. Their unique approach on assisting you to build your own brand, determine your products that suit you and coach you through mindset and the logistics needed to set up an online business is what keeps us clear on our vision and mission and focussed on what our next step is. Although the overall elements that are out there to approach your audience online are general the way you can do it and the mix that suits you best are unique. Rhonda keeps you sharp in staying through to your why, your business ethics and your brand.

You make a decision using your brain when choosing to work with someone, however a lot of it is also gut feeling. When the combination tells you to go for it, the difficult part of surrender to the knowledge of your guru/coach will play a big part. This has to do with trust. Based on that trust we have taken steps, invested in logistics or marketing that were not fully clear to us at that moment. We are convinced that because of this, the start-up phase of our business is going much faster than it would have, had we figured it out all by ourselves. Because of the strategic branding sessions with Rhonda we are clear on what our brand stands for, who our audience is and what value we add to their lives. Rhonda's coaching doesn't only grow your business, it also grows you. The personal development that comes from interacting with her and the approach of earning your money with your passion are immense.

Love Inge Hart

BRANDit
START EVERYDAY WITH
A PRAYER AND
A SMILE

19

How To Be An Unstoppable Family With Children!

So you can have read all about our lives and our travels around the world. I have highlighted for you the business side of things and how it has impacted Brian and I - but many people out there are still asking about Hanalei and the practicalities of world travel with a child.

Because I don't want you to feel as though I have left anything out of this book I am going to speak about Hanalei and the practicalities of world travel and global business with her in toe.

Honestly though it is not something we think about regularly or something that Hanalei finds stressful or different. This has always been her life so it is just normal for her. What you show your kids is normal is normal to them!

WHAT IS IMPORTANT TO AN EXPAT/TRAVELING CHILD?

When it comes to traveling the world with a child the things that don't seem important to you are the pinnacle of existence for them. For example, knowing that Santa will be able to find them is a big deal for a child and something that you and we might take for granted because we are in on the whole big secret. However, you want to keep a child's life as normal and secure as possible you need to listen to their thoughts, feelings, concerns, and ideas. You may want to consider always going back to a familiar place for the holidays, or writing letters to Santa that he responds to assure your child that he knows where they are at all times. It is the little things that make the biggest difference.

Kids are inquisitive beings - so it is essential that you research as much as possible about the places you are going with your children to they can know as much about the new culture as possible. Look at things from a child's perspective and highlight tasty fruits, dangerous spiders, foods that they might like. Teach them how to say easy phrases, so they fit in as soon as you get there.

When we moved to Fiji with Hanalei, she was like a minor celebrity. We looked radically different to the rest of the people in rural Fiji, and kids have a healthy curiosity about things and individuals that are different. A three-year-old little girl with blonde hair and blue eyes drew plenty of looks. But kids at that age are just kids; there is no judgment or fears just a need to see something foreign to them.

One of the best ways to include your children into their new culture is get them involved in the games or sport that other children like to play. Hanalei met a little girl and her Mum at the Beach in Mexico and while the girls were playing she asked if Hanalei wanted to join in a local ballet class. We joined them for ballet for six weeks at a small local church, and it was one of the best experiences for both of us.

Expat Exchange is a wealth of information - there is stuff about relocating, schooling and how to adjust to a new environment from people who have already done it. If you want to make your transition as seamless as possible, I suggest you research heavily before you move anywhere.

One of the biggest things about moving and traveling around the world is the school aspect. You will find some schools where they speak English have other expats that speak

English too. However, you don't want your kids to only speak English and impose their English words on their friends continually, so it is important that you allow your children to learn some local words as well.

Even a six-month stay in a place can leave an impression on your child, and they can form an appreciation for the way non-English speaking worlds run. This type of education gives your child a sense of power even in a completely foreign situation - throughout their whole life. For Hanalei, it was difficult and frustrating at first because she was shy, however, once she saw us learning too and her friends trying to learn English she embraced it completely and loved to speak Spanish and hear other people speaking Spanish to her.

Schooling for Expat Kids

Your choices for longer stays usually include:

- an international school
- the local school
- homeschooling

The familiarity of English and the curriculum are the benefits of the international school system. Most countries have American schools, and if not, then the UK system comes a close second. While we were in Spain, we opted for a British International School with Spanish as the second language taught.

In Panama, Hanalei attended Tangerine Education Center for expat children with a split English/Spanish curriculum.

The first time we lived in Bali, Hanalei attended Bali International School in Jimbaran area, closer to the Bukit Peninsula. Although she was quite young [2 years] she still had the opportunity to attend a 4 hrs a day kids interaction class with children from all over the world.

We moved back to Bali in July 2015, this time we chose Sunrise School, in Seminyak for Hanalei. We love their philosophy on teaching and their motto "Think Globally, Act Locally, and Be Totally." They have kinder all the way to high school.

When we lived in Tenerife, Spain Hanalei Attended Callao Learning Center for six months. Another small, International School that focuses on the British Curriculum but offers an open source style learning that is personalized more to the child with small classrooms of under 20 kids.

Your kids can mix with other expat children, and their local classmates are the perfect way for your kids to find out what the country is really like.

But because of the exclusive nature of most of these schools, some parents take the local option. If your kids are younger and not facing exams, then this could be a great experience for them with guaranteed local friends.

Up until this year, we have had the luxury of finding private international schools for Hanalei to attend before she started "real" school. She was able to drop right in and interact and learn from the children even if the language was not English.

Hanalei has attended school in Bali with very little English spoken, Peru with no English, Brazil with only Portuguese,

Spain with both English and Spanish and Panama with both English and Spanish.

I can tell you; she has never once complained about not understanding or feeling frustrated. Play has no language barrier. I do believe this year, being 1st grade it was necessary for her to be taught in English as the primary language. This way she was learning to read and write in her native language and have Spanish as the secondary.

The third option is home-schooling, which is easier than ever before, with so much support online. Home-schooling is a good choice in countries where enrollment can be a challenge or if you are moving around for more frequently.

For the last eight years, we have been staying in one location for 4-6 months, and she would change schools as we moved. Now that she is in 4th grade we made the decision to stay in one place for the school year and take "mini-vacations" during the year, because Hanalei told us she did not want to homeschool. She likes attending schools and meeting children her age.

So it is very important to listen to the needs of your child when traveling abroad and choosing their education.

Expat Kids Love Life!

Don't stress too much. Most expat kids are incredibly well-adjusted and have friends all over the globe. They get to visit worlds that most teenagers just see on television and are comfortable with traveling in a way many older people only dream about.

Hanalei has the biggest heart and the most open mind I have ever seen in a child or an adult for that matter. She is in love with learning new things and meeting new people. Traveling has made the world so small in her eyes, and she believes she can and will see every country on the globe because they are just a plane trip away.

But it's not just about travel; these kids tend to be more tolerant than children raised in only one culture. They do not judge color or race. They grow up understanding compassion and empathy without judgment. They look at the world as a beautiful place, not a place of war or destruction.

STEPS TO INSTILLING VALUES IN YOUR CHILD

One of the most important things your child can do is to internalize the values they will live by.

~ Unstoppable Momma

For moms, dads, and other parenting adults, this process can be both rewarding and terrifying.

On the one hand, we see children expressing their honesty, compassion, and other positive values that we would hope to pass on to them.

On the other hand, they often also do things that don't reflect our values—or even that contradict our deeply held values.

Other influences in their lives—peers, media, other adults—can influence them to adopt values and perspectives that we may not share. We may feel like it's out of our hands. But it's not.

Even though it's critical that young people internalize their own values (rather than having them imposed), parenting adults continue to shape and influence their children's values throughout the teenage years and into adulthood. The goal and challenge for parents is to help teens "make their own" the kinds of values that help them make positive choices throughout their lives.

Moving from external control (such as doing what your parent says you should do) to self-regulation (doing what you believe in doing) is a central task of growing up, particularly during the teenage years.

UNSTOPPABLE STEPS TO INSTILL VALUES IN YOUR CHILD

- **NURTURE A WARM RELATIONSHIP**

Children tend to be more willing to accept and internalize parental values when they feel close to their parents. And close families usually have many shared interests and values that reinforce each other.

- **SHOW AND TELL WHAT MATTERS**

A key to your influence on your child's values is that they understand what really matters to you. The best way to do that is both to show and tell—help them see the values in action in your own life, then talk about why you do what you do.

Getting the child's attention, being clear, and regularly reinforcing the values all help children to more accurately understand the values you hope for them. That increases the likelihood that they will internalize those values.

- **CULTIVATE OPEN COMMUNICATION**

Teens are more likely to internalize their parents' values when they have open, frequent, and honest communication with each other—when teens feel comfortable talking with their parents about tough issues and about things that matter to them.

Open communication increases the odds that teens will listen to and internalize their parents' values. In addition, parents gain a greater understanding of how their teens think and what's important to them. That makes it easier to connect the parents' values with the teens' own emerging values. I learned this from the Celestine Prophesies in the chapter for creating vision.

PAY ATTENTION TO YOUR CHILD'S WORLD AND INTERESTS

When you show interest in the things that matter to your child, you show them that you care about their choices and activities. That attentiveness, in turn, motivates your child to pay attention to and accept your values and expectations.

GIVE YOUR CHILD CHOICES AND APPROPRIATE INDEPENDENCE

Helping children see that they have power in their own lives and can influence others helps them be aware of and internalize their own values. If parents don't give choices or don't see their children as unique individuals, the children may end up pushing away in order to develop their own sense of who they are.

PROVIDE APPROPRIATE INFORMATION, GUIDELINES, AND STRUCTURES

In addition to giving children opportunities to make their own choices, it is just as important to set clear and fair expectations and consequences, then follow through with the consequences when needed. There is, however, a careful balance.

If the rules and consequences lead to feelings of being pressured or controlled, they can become counterproductive, with teens rebelling against them.

LEARN FROM YOUR CHILDREN

Your relationship with your child is a two-way street. They learn from you; you learn from them. Through their experiences, they may develop values and beliefs that enrich your life and help you see the world and other people in new ways. Be open to what they have to teach you. In the process, they will be open to what you have to teach them.

Align values with the other parent (when applicable). Shared values between parents or parenting adults increase the likelihood that their children will accept their value priorities. If values are not shared, the child may feel conflicting loyalties in picking which values to adopt as her or his own.

CULTIVATE SKILLS TO PUT VALUES INTO PRACTICE

In order to internalize values, teens skills to help her or him be confident in standing up for what they believe and to take actions based on their values. Building assertiveness and resistance skills, as well as skills of empathy, caring, and compassion, all help to reinforce positive values by putting them into action.

PROVIDE EXPERIENCES THAT REINFORCE POSITIVE VALUES AND COMMITMENTS

If caring for others is important, give young people opportunities to care for others. If being honest is important, give them opportunities to be honest. If being generous is important, give them opportunities to share. If being responsible is important, give responsibilities to the child where others are depending on her or him. When you do, also be sure to talk about or reflect on the experience, so they become more articulate about why they do what they do.

VIEW MISTAKES AS TEACHABLE MOMENTS

Your child is going to make mistakes and not live up to your values or his or her own. Sometimes those mistakes are fairly trivial; sometimes they have momentous consequences. In each case, remember to keep your relationship with your child as a priority, and seek to find ways to learn from the mistakes. Think together through appropriate consequences as well as alternate strategies for dealing with the issue in the future. That may take time, but it can pay off in the long run.

RECOGNIZE THE LIMITS

Even though you can (and do) influence your child's values, you don't control them. There's nothing parents can or should do that simply "copies" their own values onto their kids. For better and worse, many factors also influence the values teens internalize. That can include media, friends, teachers, coaches, and celebrities.

It can also include world events that sear values and priorities into young people's consciousness. So your children won't necessarily see the values you share as being as important as you see them. Indeed, they may choose to reject some values that are really important to you. That doesn't mean you have failed; it means they are becoming their own person.

So there you have it. Hanalei is a beautiful well-adjusted child. As long as you listen to them and communicate as a family you have nothing to fear about becoming world travellers and global citizens with your kids.

SUMMARY

The journey did not start here nor has it ended, it's just part of this journey that we now call Life.

One simple decision 11 years ago that was scary and nearly unrealistic, forced me into the mindset of creating my own reality.

Many may look at this picture and think "there is no way my life can be this way."

I know because I thought the same until I believed it was possible and took deliberate steps each day until the reality was greater than my fear.

Taking personal responsibility was the first step. Learning skills that seem like a foreign language, investing in my knowledge to become self-reliant then putting it into action.

This is one of the hardest roads I've ever taken but one of the most fulfilling and rewarding.

Life is meant to be lived ... no reason to wait.

#Beunstoppable

Image I posted in FaceBook on 26 September 2016 - the day we lost power in our villa - it's a hard life :)

As I finish writing this book, Hanalei is swimming in the pool and playing with our puppies as I watch her from my day lounge and Brian will be finishing his daily surf. We will then head out on our scooters for a healthy lunch before putting the finishing touches to an event we have coming up. We are so excited to be meeting many of our clients and spending quality time together having fun and working on their brands.

So now it is time for you to make that DECISION, what do you want in your life, do you know there is so much more out there for you too, all you have to do is DECIDE.

I invite you to come and join us to find out how you can take the steps to do what it is you want to create for yourself and your family, by taking in massive amount of free bonus materials supporting you and what you have read here. If you haven't already done so, go to the web address below to access them right now, and I so look forward to meeting you soon, either virtually or in person.

www.unstoppablemomma.com/bonus

Rhonda x

The Places We've Called Home

November 25 2016 will start our 9th year of travel around the world. Number 8 has always been my favorite number, playing softball, I had 8 etched in the back of my head, and it's just always been my favorite number. I declared in 2015, that was the year of my 8, that was my coming out of network marketing of being an affiliate of other companies, and taking on my own self, my own identity, my own brand, my Rhonda Swan The Unstoppable Momma personal brand and there were so many different funny things. I was 42 that year, 2015 adds up to 8, Hanalei was 8, so many great things. Then 2016 came and I thought ooh this is the year of the double 8 because there's so much more happening because the year of the 8 built up and it's the year of the double 8. And so this year is really significant of our travels. The places that our journey has taken us has been rather beautiful.

We started in Hanalei Bay, Hawaii the very first day, which was 25 November and we celebrated our 5th wedding anniversary on the 28th and we celebrated Hanalei's very first time there, and we celebrated the start of our very new life with the 3 of us, which is exactly where we started our life together, the 2 of us, 5 years before. From there we went to Porto Escondido, Mexico where we stayed two different times for 3 months then we went to Costa Rica for 2 months, Peru 3 months, Panama 3 different times had incredible family in Panama, we met people who are now life-long friends, Bocas del Toro is a very small little island, with about 2000 people just off the coast of Panama City. You fly a very small puddle jumper plane, and arrive in a big soccer field in the middle of the island. Bicycles are the main form of transport along with boats. Here you take a boat to your greatest favorite restaurant and here is where we met many people who we still consider family and some of our friends.

We lived in Nicaragua, Brazil for 5 months, Spain, Canary Islands, Paris, Belgium, Netherlands, Bali twice, Morocco, Germany, South Africa, Australia, New Zealand, Dubai, Bahrain, Bangladesh, Hong Kong, Singapore, Malaysia and Thailand have been part of our travels around the world. And all of the people that we have met have formed the fiber of our family. When you travel you find that you are so much more open, you get the best of the best of people. You meet them in their best state, a lot of them are travellers and you find communities of people that are very different that are traveling because they have no family.

So you begin to rely on your unit of expatriates and travellers because they're in the same position as you. And being a traveling family was interesting because you don't see many traveling families at all, because of course everyone thinks it's difficult to travel with kids. We met amazing people all over the world, and people who'd seen us on FaceBook or in social media or in our videos, even in places like Morocco we had people coming up to us 'Wow Untstoppable Family, it's great to meet you!' People in Paris recognizing who we are because of our online presence and that also gives more reason for you to have your Brand and really making it clear, because the clearer your brand is and the more consistent you are, you will be recognized.

And so our travels have taken us and connected us to some of the most beautiful people, it has fulfilled our wanderlust desires of adventure, Brian and I both being Geminis' easily get bored, so it's allowed us to meet new people, new cultures and to experience life in a way that we could not have in our home towns of Michigan and Chicago or in San Diego. So travel for us has not only been a blessing but it's also been a medicine for our souls.